I'LL
BE
YOUR
MIRROR

I'LL BE YOUR MIRROR

Essays & Aphorisms

DAVID LAZAR

Illustrated by Heather Frise

University of Nebraska Press | Lincoln & London

Acknowledgments for the use of copyrighted
material appear on page ix, which constitutes
an extension of the copyright page.

Library of Congress
Cataloging-in-Publication Data
Names: Lazar, David, 1957– author.
Title: I'll be your mirror:
essays and aphorisms / David Lazar.
Other titles: I will be your mirror
Description: Lincoln:
University of Nebraska Press, 2017. |
Identifiers: LCCN 2017017417 (print)
LCCN 2017033183 (ebook)
ISBN 9781496202062 (paperback: alk. paper)
ISBN 9781496205186 (epub)
ISBN 9781496205193 (mobi)
ISBN 9781496205209 (pdf)
Subjects: | BISAC: LITERARY
COLLECTIONS / Essays.
Classification: LCC PS3612.A973 (ebook) | LCC
PS3612.A973 A6 2017 (print) | DDC 814/.6—dc23
LC record available at https://
lccn.loc.gov/2017017417

Designed and set in Arno Pro by L. Auten.

For Lois

and in memory of Stephen Zamora

CONTENTS

ACKNOWLEDGMENTS

I am most grateful to the John Simon Guggenheim Foundation for a fellow-ship that allowed me to complete this book.

Many thanks to the editors and magazines in which some of these essays first appeared:

The Normal School: "To the Reader, Sincerely" (printed in *After Montaigne: Contemporary Essayists Cover the Essays*, ed. Lazar and Madden [Athens: University of Georgia Press]); and "When I'm Awfully Low: On Singing."

River Teeth: "Five Autobiographical Fragments, or She May Have Been a Witch."

Superstition Review: "Lollipop Is Mine."

Bellingham Review: "Ann; Death and the Maiden."

The Rumpus: "Pandora and the Naked Dead Woman."

Essay Review: "Hydra: I'll Be Your Mirror."

Essay Daily: "A Conversation with Robert Burton," "Meet Montaigne."

TheConversant.org: "Voluptuously, Expansively, Historically, Contradictorily: Essaying the Interview with Mary Cappello and David Lazar."

My thanks to:

Cathleen Calbert, Mary Cappello, William Fraser, Adrienne Kalfopoulou, Nicole Kirk, Delmore Lazar, Leo and Roz Lazar, Patrick Madden, Martin McGovern, Alyce Miller, Laura Oros, Lia Purpura, Jean Walton, Lois Zamora.

My intense gratitude to Heather Frise, whose drawings grace this volume and continue to inspire and unsettle me.

I would also like to thank Alicia Christensen, my editor at Nebraska, for inspiring the shape of this book, and the other editors and staff for their excellent work.

To the cast and crew, I appreciate your professionalism and your dedication to this show—I knew we wouldn't close on the road.

—DAVID LAZAR

Thanks to all those who have encouraged me to draw over the years: my mother, my sister, my daughter, and my dear friends. Also my late grandfather Jimmie Frise, whose fine cartoons have inspired me in more ways than I'm sure I even know. And of course, David, for his poetry and faith.

—HEATHER FRISE

BRIGADOON
BOWLING

After tea it's back to painting—a large poplar at dusk with a gathering storm. From time to time instead of this evening painting session I go bowling in one of the neighboring villages, but not very often.

—GUSTAV KLIMT

ANN; DEATH AND THE MAIDEN

When O.J. Simpson was leading the police on the errant chase on that freeway in LA, I was in Madison Square Garden in New York, at the famous Knicks playoff game where the monitors switched to the chase, to our astonishment, but it didn't register as surreally or wildly as it might have otherwise because I had been in the middle of telling my brother about Ann.

I was a young professor, thirty-seven, and she was an older doctoral student, thirty-four, and we had fallen for each other, and I thought it was going to be a big deal, in the way you know that someone is going to come into your life and the tectonics are going to change. I thought she might just be the girl for me, excuse the language, and was all aquiver in telling my brother the news, must have felt, I suppose in thinking back on it now, rather certain about my feelings, and about *it*, which is to say the prospects of where this new thing was headed.

Ann killed herself about a year and a half ago. The details are vague because no one seems terribly willing to yield them up. She had attempted suicide a few years before, slitting her wrists, but she was discovered or didn't quite go through with it—I'm not quite remembering which. It was serious enough for hospitalization—terrible, terrible, but not life-threatening, at least not the cuts.

She had been on a downward trajectory for years.

I haven't been able to quite stop thinking about her or to quite think about her since I heard about her death: the once promising career, writing about Virginia Woolf, that heavy eastern Kentucky accent, laden with irony and graceful goodwill. Her extraordinary recklessness. Her generosity. A bit like Zelda Fitzgerald gone in self-immolation. She was manic-depressive, as probably was Zelda. She looked a bit like Zelda, gamine and dark eyed. When I say I haven't been able to quite think about her, I mean that as much as she comes into my mind, a kind of creaturely sharp pain accompanies the thought of her, and I jump away as though I had laid my hand on a hot stove.

Twenty years ago an affaire de coeur between a professor and a graduate student not her or his own was not much of a deal in many places. In some places, geographical outposts, even encouraged. Younger, post-Internet readers perhaps won't quite understand the human urgencies of being alone and being isolated among rolling hills and aging colleagues in the earlier days of academe. To this sector of audience, the emotional premise of my memory might seem politically nauseating. What can I say except I understand, times change, etc. People communed where possible, even when the tincture of taboo tinted the edges of relation. They still do.

We met furtively at first, after a series of notes she had sent me toward the end of a seminar. We did meet, I must stress, after the seminar ended. But, and I suppose this is among the reasons I turn to writing these things, to see what repressed details show their hoary heads, I remember now that she was actually separated and moving toward a divorce from her third husband. But they hadn't actually, which is to say formally, made plans to divorce yet. That, no doubt, was part of our film noirish meetings in back alleys and cheap motels. It was one thing to date an available graduate student of one's own age. Quite another to be perceived (albeit wrongly) as a homewrecker, sharpest edge of a triangle.

We decided to go for a road trip. We would go to Louisville, Kentucky, to see George Carlin and stay in the Brown Hotel. What could be more alluring: how could I refuse a hotel whose history contains Lily Pons, Al Jolson, Marie of Romania, and Joan Crawford? I was hooked. I remember nothing of the drive there. And I do remember George Carlin then (this would have been around 1995) as harsh, funny, brilliant. I loved all his phases, even his dark, more existentially accusatory last phase. The drive back from Louisville to Athens, Ohio, was kaleidoscopically strange. Ann talked, virtually without pause, for the entire ten hours. I remember trying, at various times, to get a word, a question, a pithy aside, in, to virtually no avail. She was the Louisville Southern Railroad, and nothing was going to derail her. At the end of ten completely confusing hours, I felt like my head was going to explode; we finally made it back to my house in Ohio. Ann crashed, badly. Inconsolable, on my bed, she could only speak about the blackness of the world and how miserably unnecessary most things in life were.

Well, the virtue of love, one supposes, is sympathy. I didn't bail as she told me that she was bipolar since of course that was beyond her control, and she had been the person I had fallen for, which the scary blip in the car didn't seem to have altered. But a second item concerned me more: she had been prescribed lithium but didn't want to take it because she put on weight on lithium. As she put it in her eastern Kentucky accent, "Honey, it makes my stomach all poochy." I never liked that last word; it sounded like she had a small dachshund in there.

This was before the flood of memoirs, articles, etc., . . . about bipolarity, so I was only vaguely aware of what it meant. I imagine I looked it up. I know we talked about it quite a bit, Ann and me. I also know that she was adamant about not treating it clinically, despite her own misgivings about doing so. Like many manic-depressives, she was more than a little addicted to her mania, despite the price she paid with her depression. I have hundreds of pages of letters that she wrote to me—this was still the era of physical correspondence, and Ann was both intellectually and emotionally engaged with the epistle, Woolf's, Millay's, her own, and would pour out letter after letter to me, really lovely missives at first, before, over the three years we spent together, they turned first melancholy, then accusatory, occasionally incoherent, at times, rarely, strange, spooky. While never explicitly self-threatening, there was a just-wasn't-made-for-these-times, shouldn't-be-here note she would hit, which would give me chills. When we would reconcile, she would laugh it all off: "Honey, don't make too much of it."

It's almost too painful to admit this, but I had a glimmer that she was dead from Facebook. This was about two years ago, and she and I hadn't spoken for about a year but had thrown a few messages back and forth about how we were overdue, as though we were desultory library books that someone had forgotten to levy fines on. A post on her web page had struck a valedictory note that gave me pause, and there hadn't been any other posts for a long time. I'll tell you exactly what I did: I went to Google and typed in Ann _____ obituary, and it came right up, the details of her death, the service in Ashland, Kentucky, at the Lazar funeral home. I really did think I had snapped for a moment. Then, what's a Lazar doing in Ashland, Kentucky? As they say, as we say, you can't write this stuff. But more to the point, there was that sudden feeling that something is missing in the world that you suspected had been missing in the world. It isn't quite confirmation; it's more like a very sudden and ruthless sense that your teenaged angst-ridden feeling that absolutely nothing mattered was completely to the point. A feeling of nothingness, absolute degree zero.

Things started to fall apart between us rather quickly. Rather than take her lithium, Ann self-medicated with drinking. And I'll tell you, I joined the party. We drank like the proverbial fishes. There were wonderful nights. Lots of sex, lots of talk. Lots of music and dancing. But also: lots of *Who's Afraid of Virginia Woolf?* After a while I think we refined bitter repartee down to the point where Albee had nothing on us. We even had the missing child, since I very much wanted one, and she couldn't have one and refused to consider the idea of adopting one. And what would any relationship purgatory be without a parade of others? I think Ann knew, fairly early, that her instability was difficult for me to hold onto. So, like any R(r)omantic, she went all out to make things impossible.

Polymorphous Ann, in a state you'd kiss a telephone pole while looking over your shoulder to see if I were witnessing it in sorrow or pain. Can you imagine the scenes? Have you versions of your own? They were intense and recriminatory and full of a sense of the inevitable. I remember trudging off to a party one night after a particularly cute ronde of accusations, whose against whose escapes me, but we were determined to socialize in the way that younger people think that socializing while miserable is part of some dark gospel of experience. Our general dark economy of failure and heartbreak meant that I could usually get the better of her (though just) through daggers of insinuation and insult, whereas she would always one up me through behavioral outrageousness. In short, no matter what I would *say* to try to and let some of the blood drain from my wounds (and in the process from her heart), she could *do* something to wound me further, deeper, more painfully. At this particular party (which could have been Anyparty) no sooner did I have my coat off, reaching, rather desperately, for my first drink of the night— there, I should specify—than I noted one of my colleague's arms around her, stroking her back, her head leaning toward or into him. Feeling my gaze—the point, of course—she turned and gave me one of those looks, or rather, not one of, because I think of it as distinctly hers, so heartbreaking was it, so incapable was I of responding to it at the time, a look that would have done Henry James proud, part hopeful and part self-loathing, part pleading and part lower-grade spite. In the spirit of sinking to the occasion, I shrugged a shoulder and turned away, walked off. Is there such a thing as having the final gesture? What's final, after all? I suppose when I spotted them making out in his car later that night I might have asked the same question.

Writing this makes me queasy, I hope for obvious reasons. Not because I care particularly about giving details about my own brazen bad behavior. Well, brazen? I was in the middle of an insoluble dilemma, seeing a wild, wonderful woman who wouldn't control her demons, her mis-chemistry.

If ever anyone I've known had a sense of determinism, a fatalistic sense that things were going to go badly, it was Ann. In this, however, or the way she carried this, she was very *nouvelle vague*-ish, very light on the *we're all damned so let's all have a damn good time*. She managed to pull it off because she meant it, because she was sincere. It didn't come across as a superficial quality, her carpe diem. And I'm not reading backward from her death. I'm reading backward from a closely remembered sense that her death was waiting up ahead, not very far up ahead, for her to be cast in its light. She was a postmortem avant la lettre but with a kind of wicked gaiety. It you've never been around anyone who created that kind of dark vortex, of wit and energy, of the world as our own small apocalypse just waiting to collapse on us, of the contradictory pressures of having to actually succeed at something colliding with a sense of the utter temporal meaninglessness of trying to do much of anything, you may have some sense of the cosmic charge of their pull, why that hand of theirs reaching out of the whirlpool seems more attractive as a way to be pulled in than as a moral imperative to save the drowning, though that, too, is listed on your day's list of things to do. But when they hand you your glass of bourbon and sit in your lap and say, "So, honey, let's talk about us and *Orlando* and the end of the world," you're hard-pressed not to set your stopwatch to Finis. This was her effect on me, a sense of not caring about consequence or time. It was liberating and horrifying, destructive, intense.

We really liked each other. We were quite hot for each other. After some dark night of the relational soul, when things were said that never should have been thought and one of us had threatened to leave for our cars, after three or seven martinis or shots of Jack Daniels—rather vain threat, or was it? those were the days when I still might have done something that stupid—she would break the tension with a sexual tease, some honey-dripped request to scratch her back, or she would merely start laughing, which would infect my infected rage and break it.

One time she came with me back to New York, a family visit, and we planned a day walking around the city, museums and such. She wore high black heels, which I suggested was a bad idea. "Honey, I can't walk around New York in anything less than stylish shoes." By the end of the day, she couldn't walk, feet cramped, I—well, I was younger and full of reasons to be pissed off. You can be angry about anything if you're tending toward anger with someone. Nothing much will make you angry if you don't want to be angry. Oh, the delightful perquisites of age. I was annoyed as she walked barefoot down Sixth Avenue toward Penn Station, an image I now find equally winsome, delightful, heartbreaking. My own inability, at the time, to be charmed, though I haven't the slightest doubt I wanted to be and wouldn't let myself, is beyond unnerving. And you can't reminisce apologetically with her. But to whom am I speaking, other than a sentimentally guilty conscience?

One year I gathered my family in Ohio for Thanksgiving, the only time we've been together for the holiday in the thirty-five years since my mother's death. This detail overweighs the story from the outset, but that was my experience. I cooked everything, for fifteen people. I should have known trouble lay ahead. I mean, how many movies had I seen? My father and his wife arrived first, and a freak snowstorm hit. They decided to walk in the picturesque paths near my house; except that five feet away from the house, my father's wife slipped and broke her wrist. Emergency room. Weekend in pain.

Ann arrived with a good head start on being pickled. That part's okay—I drink during the holidays. Sometimes I think the best thing about the holidays is an excuse for having a drink in the afternoon. Sometimes I don't need an excuse for having a drink in the afternoon, but during the holidays it's like a free pass. But Ann started hitting the bourbon hard after that. My most vivid memory of the day was of being in the kitchen, adjacent to the dining room, where everyone had started gathering, and cracking the door to see what was up. Ann was sitting astraddle a chair, skirt hitched up, and I caught her saying, to my father, REALLY LOUDLY, "I don't see the problem with my dating a Jew."

I closed the door and grabbed a bottle myself. The only other thing I remember is getting her a ride home early and a slightly wounded expression she gave me—kind of toasted, sardonic and hurt.

Why am I writing about Ann? Why am I thinking about Ann? Guilt is a privilege of the living. And it's certainly one of my defaults, one of the feelings I leap toward, or is it crawl into? whenever pressed, even when or perhaps especially when the pressing is internal. An old familiar and, yes, in some ways an easy one. I've always argued that going toward darker feelings too quickly, too easily, is just as sentimental as Hallmark brightness. Why do I feel so automatically guilty about Ann, why, for example, in this essay, while mentioning her wildness, her mania, skimming over what became a kind of tic toward betrayal ("I only fuck you over because I love you so much, and I'm afraid I can't really have you"), do I feel like I betrayed *her*, that I'm somehow responsible for the hole I feel in the world, the absence of her, even though we were not so much in touch?

It isn't that we were not so much in touch. Nor do I think I'm suffering from the delusion that I could have "saved" her, though I may be in a bit of denial about that. After we broke up, I had one of my scariest dreams ever. I was in my house, with the woman I was going to marry (rather quickly) and later divorce (rather belatedly), and dreamed that Ann was something like a witch, or perhaps a daemon, a very powerful and dark spirit who was trying to break into, or gain entry into, the house. The entire house was surrounded by the suffocating air of her presence, and the door was creaking at her hot breath, which would melt the locks. Should she enter, terrible things would happen. That's what so awful about the dream, the lack of specificity—terrible, terrible things would happen, like I had never experienced before, and all would become horror and loss.

Just as the door was giving way, I woke up. And the house was quiet, and the woman next to me was quietly sleeping. Ann was miles away, presumably in her bed. The woman next to me would cause me much more harm than the figure in my dreams.

But Ann figured for me . . . as a loss of control. I have managed, barely, to keep things together through the years of my adult life—doing all the things one needs to do. And I think the face I show to the world is a very functional one. Yet I frequently feel as though I were a breath away from losing it, and I've wondered all my adult life what it would be like to let all caution, all responsibility, all care for self and public esteem, go. I seem to have gravitated frequently to people who were very irresponsible. My dear friend Tony, dead this spring of a heart attack—and he just a month younger than I—spent much of the last thirty years wearing down his body with vodka. First he was just drinking a lot. Then he was married with kids and was passing out in the street. There were interventions, rehabs, and he couldn't keep a job or finish his degree, and he just kept falling and falling and breaking things and turning his insides into a stew. And he died alone of a heart attack in a motel in Vermont a few months ago. He called me drunk all the time. He called all his friends drunk all the time. We stopped taking the calls because who had the time to hear Tony go on and on and not listen to a word you'd said? But he'd sober up, and we'd talk, and I'd see him when I went to New York, at his apartment on Ninth Street.

Once I tried to surprise him on New Year's Eve. The doorman shook his head and waved me in. Tony's doorway was ajar, and I found him naked on the floor, moaning like Caliban, looking like Caliban, bloated and dirty. I got him covered and over to the sofa. We talked for a bit. And I said, "Tony, you have to clean up." That was it. As messed up as he was, he threw me out.

But we talked a few days later. When you know someone for decades, it's like that.

Have I been a flaneur of some of my own darkest impulses with some of my friends and a woman I've loved, being close enough to my own worst-case scenarios to feel their hot breath while watching others take the heat? That would be too hard on myself, and thus too easy, though it's also not completely untrue as my own psychic précis.

After Ann and I moved into *a post-relationship but still who knows what's going on* state, I was in a rather dark place. I may have left a lot of bottles at her place, but I hardly left the bottle. Trying not to hit something in the road (like a projection of her face over Myrna Loy's? or a vision of her walking into a room with her cheekbones flaring?), I flipped my car three times and almost died. I was on my way to a liaison with another woman, but I had them call her and my best friend from the hospital. Apparently, I do have a bit of a problem with guilt. When the doctor came to sew up the cut over my eye, I told him not to use any anesthesia (I was still in shock). They all looked at me like I was mad.

Occasionally, after a cooling-down period, while I still lived in Ohio, I would meet Ann for lunch. And then she moved back to Kentucky, too distracted to keep working on the PhD, got a job at a high school, was fired. We talked on the phone occasionally. She was funny, incredibly sweet, every time sounding a little more broken. She'd always say that her craziness with me was her biggest regret, which was, I think, supposed to make me feel better but somehow always made me feel worse.

Ann, I think, felt the sting of her lost promise. As I and a few of the people who loved her do. But disappointing oneself is worse than anything else. She fled to Florida, was seeing a considerably older physician, in whose bathroom, apparently, she attempted to cut her wrists. She survived with a sense of ignominy added on to everything else.

She would always ask about my son and with a genuine interest and sweetness that made me think of her insistence that she didn't want children. But then I have to remind myself that there is a difference between not wanting children and thinking oneself incapable of raising them. Most of the people I know who are choosing childlessness are doing so because they simply do not want children, a perfectly respectable choice, if one inimical to my own essential emotional character. If anything in my life has given me consistent joy and satisfaction, it's child rearing. I've arguably been a bit of a washout at relationships, at least romantic relationships. But I seem to be pretty good at the parenting thing.

Ann, however, thought herself an impossible mother. I forget that. And I think at the time of our relationship I fused or confused that belief with her having some hostility to kids. Absurd. She was lovely with kids. But in her imagination she would have ended up the crazy mother, incapable of caring for her charge or charges. Who knows which of our decisions are sane, self-knowing appraisals of our shortcomings, and which are self-rationalizing justifications of what we really want? Half the time they overlap. Or as Yogi Berra might say, "Half the time they're 75 percent the same thing."

We talked, but then there were gaps. I'm sure you can traipse through your own spotty relational paths, filled with friendship sinkholes in which people you care about manage nevertheless to disappear, drop away for periods of time as you attend to your children, your books, your winter clothes, and your mortgages. It was during a fall, a winter, when I was listlessly trying to get in touch with her that I found out there would be no more getting in touch with her. This is a new category of social experience, the Facebook memento mori, and it makes me queasy, I must say, the way pages linger on after death like newspaper stories from the past that people can make continual addenda to, but why? . . . I understand the argument that they remain as monuments of a sort, although, I think, of a rather desultory sort. An editor of mine lingers on in my contacts after death, as do Ann and one or two others, their pages a form of accidental literary cryogenics.

Someone had written something on Ann's page about not forgetting her. That's what sent me racing to the obituaries, marked with my own name.

I've been listening to "Death and the Maiden" as I write this. I listen to Schubert a reasonable amount, the *Winterreise*, the *Impromptus* . . . and I was reminded of how much I loved the Quintet in D minor recently when I was watching *Crimes and Misdemeanors* with my son. It's so muscular in its tragic overtones and so unrelenting in its oceanic grief, its continually enlarging beauty of unknowing that signifies the end, which is the end of music. The motif began as early as 1517, in Hans Baldung Grien's "Death and the Maiden," a mournful young woman pulled by her hair by the skeleton of doom, and then there are countless variations through the Renaissance, in the Romantic era . . . One of my favorites is Adolf Hering's "Death and the Maiden" (1900), in which the scantily clad fin de siècle nymph is in a swoon, about to be romantically devoured by the black-shrouded figure, the Ur-mourner who devours what he wants, Death as Dracula, an obvious connection, turning our fears of dissolution into, ironically, a gothic nightmare of endless life. Talk about displacement.

Speaking of displacement, in *Crimes and Misdemeanors* the difficult woman, the troubled woman, is killed by Martin Landau, the Jewish man, to the strains of "Death and the Maiden." Unlike the character of Judas, I haven't killed anyone, but ironically, while Judas realizes that he can shake off his burden of guilt in a godless world, continue with his life, his family, I find my own sense of guilt less labile, more burdensome. The older I get, the less interested I find myself in changing feelings that, even if harrowing, are still somehow true to my essential nature or some part of a series of experiences that jibe with my sense of emotional necessity. One could say I want to keep feeling them because feeling them seems emotionally right, even if neurotic in a classic sense, and thus truer to me. Does this classify them as "sentimental" according to my earlier definition? Perhaps.

I feel responsible for Ann's death, as though if she hadn't met me, she would have been better off. Yes, who can possibly know this kind of thing? Who can rewind and untangle the currents of necessity and self-determination? Who can predict the pitiless fortunes or absurd graces of those who come into and out of our orbits? Who can keep friends and lovers alive when they won't take their medicine or won't put down their bottles? Who can forgive in just the right measure and with transcendent language? Seriously, tell me—I mean it. I'm easy to find. I spend half my days sitting around waiting for a knock on the door, someone standing there with a paper full of accusations. They would always all be just.

WHEN I'M
AWFULLY LOW
On Singing

One of the first things I remember writing was part of a song, though it's rather generous to characterize it as such; I was improvising a line from an advertising jingle. I was eight years old and on my way home from Yankee Stadium in the Bronx to the far end of Brooklyn with my eleven-year-old brother. It was 1965. It seems unthinkable now, doesn't it, that an eleven-year-old and an eight-year-old would traverse the city in that way? When my fourteen-year-old son ventures out in Chicago, I put a monitoring device on him and call Pinkerton. In any case someone had a transistor radio, and it was playing a jingle for a spaghetti sauce. I remember it as this:

Tune up your taste with Romani
For flavor that is fine
And tastes so nice
It's the flavor that your favor . . .

And here I think the original line was something like "When you need a sauce to savor." It scans reasonably well. But the line that came into my eight-year-old head was "It's the flavor that you favor / When you need an amputator." I'm not sure exactly what an "amputator" might be, something that amputates, one assumes, that can amputate anything that requires amputation. It's a rather strange, a grotesque, idea, a sauce for someone who is going to have an amputation and wants something that tastes nice. I told my brother the substituted line, and he was properly amused with the "what's wrong with you" look that became a kind of calling card in my childhood for having made my mark by disturbing my brother's sensibilities. It is still a most pleasant indulgence.

Strangely, this jingle, and the substituted gothic punchline, has stayed in my consciousness for half a century. It just pops up from time to time, in faculty meetings, long airplane flights, while I'm listening attentively to someone telling me about their latest book. I think, "It's the flavor that you favor when you need an amputator." It's a way, I think, of subconsciously regaining my private interior space, a kind of siren call to the strange song world in my head and its frequently intense repetitiveness. I needed an amputator at age eight, and I suppose I always will.

Oliver Sacks, in *Musicophilia*, uses the term *earworm*, from the German *Ohrwurm*, to talk about the jingles, the musical phrases, any bit of song or music that gets stuck in the brain and repeats, doesn't dislodge immediately or so easily. Since I fall closer to the OCD spectrum than most who aren't clearly on it, my auditory sensitivity may be one of its more obvious signs.

And I think it exposes the relationship of my creative impulse to the world of song, which showed up early in the amputator jingle, which still hasn't left me. Like most of my relationships, this one is tangled and neurotic, full of satisfactions and reflections of despair. And it swirls around songs like "They Can't Take That Away from Me" and "I've Got You under My Skin" and "If I Loved You" but also "If Only Had a Brain" and "The Babbit and the Bromide." More recent songs, too, comparatively at least, like Elvis Costello's "All This Useless Beauty" and Stephen Sondheim's "Not a Day Goes By" and Stephin Merritt's "Epitaph for My Heart." As much as with any of my favorite writers over the years, Yeats or Dorothy Sayers, Montaigne or M. F. K. Fisher, Charles Lamb or Walter Benjamin, my head has been filled daily—I'm tempted to say almost constantly—by the work of Yip Harburg and Ira Gershwin, Lorenz Hart and Dorothy Fields, Stephen Sondheim, Johnny Mercer, and the respective composers, Rodgers, Kern, Arlen, Kahn . . .

But you see, I haven't just heard the songs, I sing them, and sometimes have to sing them (sometimes love to sing them) over and over for reassurance, for my place in an ongoing narrative, to make sure the song and I were still in the musical called "the real world," for the pleasure of singing, sometimes because it's just what my brain instructs me to do without much reason at all.

My mother sang me songs that I still remember—I probably remember her early singing to me better than I remember her speaking voice from many years later: "Lavender Blue" and "The Party's Over" from *The Bells Are Ringing* (it's no wonder I have a confused, eroticized relationship to Judy Holliday) and "Hush Little Baby." I sang "Lavender Blue" to my own son when he was an infant and toddler. Some of the new research in music theory, in what some researchers are calling "applied musicology," has focused on the zygonic, or imitative, nature of music in cognitive development and cultural organization. That's to say that we learn more through song and sound, how we speak, teach, and enjoy each other, in profoundly *psychomusical* interactions that we're barely aware of. Oliver Sacks writes in *Musicophilia*, "Underlying this is the extraordinary tenacity of musical memory, so that much of what is heard during one's early years may be 'engraved' on the brain for the rest of one's life." My early songs do not just linger in the brain, though—I sing them irrepressibly, an echo chamber of the past reproduced. That I've spent much of my life singing, mostly to no audience, though occasionally to a very select audience, I'm sure has its roots in the preoedipal pleasure I derived from my mother's voice. Am I trying to re-create it, find something of it in my own voice? Yeah . . . our response to song is primal, and Darwin proposed that speech was a secondary impulse to the musical one, so tied is it to the rhythms of our movement, to the excitations of our quotidian and extraordinary lives. This idea disrupts our sense of the lyrical through inversion.

I like to sing, and there was a lot of singing in my little row house when I was growing up. My mother, in her lilting soprano, would sing show tunes—mainstream stuff from Rodgers and Hammerstein, Lerner and

Loewe, Meredith Wilson, Jerome Kern, Irving Berlin, Frank Loesser. My father favored arias from Italian opera, especially Verdi and, his favorite, Puccini. He had a deep, loud bass with more than a hint of vibrato, and he would let it soar, though never for very long. It felt like a musical assault when I was very young and the music strange, less so the older I became, when the mystery behind my father's knowledge of all those arias took hold. My parents did not listen to classical music or attend performances of the opera or the symphony, so it always confused and dazzled me that my father could break out into an aria from *Madame Butterfly* or *Tosca*. He had been raised in the tenements in Brooklyn and the Bronx, and his formal education had stopped at high school. These outbursts of what seemed like high culture at high volume were a household mystery, and like many household mysteries, I never thought to ask him how he knew these songs until years later. We live with mysteries in our childhood because they become, at some point, domesticated mysteries, part of the family's zeitgeist. Decoding them never really enters the equation. It's only later (if at all), and frequently selectively, that questions fly out of us like bats from our memories or subconscious: did that really happen, and why, and how was it possible? In fact, the question of this strange knowledge on his part frequently was always swept aside by the fact that he was too loud. My father's voice was always high volume, and frequently the broadcasting of belligerence was a function I too often associated it with. So, even when it was Bellini and not belittlement at middle C, my small self in our small row house retreated. *He's going for that high note, boys, dive, dive!*

As it turned out, my father was to tell me years later, that as a boy and young man he became enamored of opera from listening to it on the radio, broadcasts of the Met, a most democratic musical amore, as it turns out. He would, whenever he could scrounge up the money, go to the old Metropolitan Opera House on Thirty-Seventh Street and buy standing room tickets in the nosebleed section. This is why I grew up with arias. When he sings now, basso profundo is a much thinner baritone. He's ninety-six and all but blind, can't see my wonder that these arias still stay with him. He hears the applause, however. "I would have loved to have been an opera singer," he says.

"Of course," he adds, "I also would have loved to have been a Rockefeller." Which one, I wonder? Rockefeller, that is.

One of my first memories is meeting a singer with my father. We were walking down Fifth Avenue in the 1950s, and we bumped into Perry Como, who greeted my father warmly. He was a huge TV star at the time, and even though I was five or so, the aura of the singer, if not his voice, rubbed off on my father.

Around the same time I heard the first song on the radio that I remember being transfixed by. It was Herman's Hermits's "Mrs. Brown, You've Got a Lovely Daughter." It was specifically the way Peter Noone, with his Mancunian accent, sang, "She's made it clear enough it ain't no good to pine," that entranced me, that made the song sound like speech, like intensified speech, before I'd ever had a thought of what a song was, how it could be used, or what any of the histories of lyricism were. *Luv* and *luvely*. So working-class. I wasn't so sure what "pining" was, but I knew it had something to do with the escapable daughter. And why was he saying all this to her *mother*? Was that . . . okay? I was pretty sure it wasn't. It confused me, and I liked it. The rhythm guitar sounded like a maudlin continuance of everyday life.

I also remember being in the car on a late afternoon in 1965. Sleepily, in the back seat, I could hear the announcer say that Nat King Cole had died. And as we drove through the newly desultory streets of Manhattan, looking for a place to park near our destination restaurant, Nat King Cole warmed up the car with "Darling, Je Vous Aime Beaucoup." I think since then I've always had a soft spot for songs that combined English and French, like "Michelle" by the Beatles and Charles Aznavour's "You Are the One for Me (Formidable)" and so many of those delightful French yé-yé songs of the sixties. Of course my favorite is probably "Never Gonna Dance" by Jerome Kern and the divine Dorothy Fields:

Though, I'm left without a penny
The wolf was discreet, he left me my feet
And so, I put them down on anything
But the la belle, la perfectly swell romance.

Of Fields and Astaire I'll have more to say later, but the movement from French to English in these songs, from the 1930s, to the 1960s, always suggests a kind of romantic borderlessness, the idea that not that many words are necessary to put love over in another tongue but that nevertheless one has to put some effort into translation in order to bridge the cultural barrier: *la belle, formidable, très bien ensemble . . .* I don't know how it sounds to French ears when an American singer mangles French (the English are generally much better), but I always find a special thrill in hearing the accents of Yves Montand or Charles Aznavour or Serge Gainsbourg or Edith Piaf singing in English. Their vowels linger longer than American singers, and their quirky inflections add unexpected emotional vicissitudes to the songs. They're good actors, which helps.

So, my parents sang, and there were songs everywhere: in the house, on the radio, in the streets, and clearly from an early age song lyrics seemed likely things to deform for my pleasure, to devour and abuse. They were pleasures to me even without my grotesque manipulations. It was important to me from very early on, when I heard a song I responded to, whether it was Sarah Vaughan on my mother's eight-track or the Carpenters on my cassette or watching Richard Kiley sing in *Man of La Mancha* from the audience in a Broadway theater, to not just hear the song but to substitute myself for the singer, to be the singer singing the song and also have the song as my own as a kind of spiritual possession, at the same time. My responses to songs were intensely emotional, and so when I found one that seemed important to me, it became a kind of totem, something that would protect me, and because of my identification with the singer, I would sing it in my mind as both myself and the singer, merged.

My first Broadway play was a musical, *Oliver*, in 1963, and we bought the LP, which I still have. I liked to sing the song "Where Is Love" in my wan boy-soprano, and my parents trotted me out at some parties to sing it, my mother beckoning me to sing the song of a boy singing for his lost mother, which would only fit me too well in a few years. I was terribly shy, but I must have thought it sounded okay because I had that queasy combination of horror and pleasure that connects so many of my intense childhood memories. There is some combination of qualities in myself I can hardly reconcile in memory: a paralyzing shyness with occasionally intense brashness, as when in an elementary school production of *Hansel and Gretel*, when I was playing the Hansel in the "B" company (we performed for the lower grades), my teacher urged me to speak louder. I walked to the front of the stage and asked the Brooklyn school crowd, "Can you hear me?" to the heart attack horror of my teacher. This was Brooklyn, and I had dangled red meat. Pandemonium ensued.

At some point I refused to continue singing "Where Is Love" publicly, perhaps when I had a budding sense of the five- or six-year-old self as ridiculous. But I can still remember the song, as I remember everything I memorized between the ages of five and twenty five, rather a lot really—songs, poems, soliloquies. I've memorized virtually nothing since, and I can barely remember a line I've written. This last assertion is more true than untrue, call it a lyrical modesty topos.

I joined the chorus in junior high school—David A. Boody Junior High School, in Brooklyn—which I remember mostly for my having allowed a very nice and tough kid who sat next to me to cheat off my tests. We had written exams—about what, I have no idea. Name three vowels in *Adeste Fideles*. He was so grateful, he put an end to the years-long bullying I had been enduring, confronting the toughest kid in the school, a little Mafioso, with me in tow. I remember that moment so clearly, standing behind him and having a power once removed, as though he were my superhero amanuensis. And all because of music and a bit of ignorance on his part. I received the Medal for Vocal Music at the end of junior high, at graduation, but I couldn't begin to tell you why. My teacher used to call me out for being out of key quite often. Perhaps I received a medal for being the least juvenile delinquent singer at Boody Junior High in Brooklyn in 1971. People have been rewarded for less, I suppose, but don't press me on this one.

In 1976 I went to my first "classical" music concert, to entertain my love affair with one of several singers I've fetishized beyond the musical delight of their voices. The concert was Dame Janet Baker's annual Carnegie Hall recital, this her twelfth. It was a signal event for me in so many ways. I had begun to listen to classical music on my own, chaotically at first, then after a couple of years in a slightly more organized and exploratory way. A great early mentor of mine had given me a stack of records—Schubert, Mahler, some baroque harpsichord stuff—and told me to just keep them and see what I liked, and I found that what I liked I liked in a very essential way, different from the essential way I loved, say, Joni Mitchell or Simon and Garfunkel. My response was completely visceral, as though I had been turning left instead of right walking down the street all these years, and turning right was the most surprising landscape. How impossible, and how silly, to have gone the same way! It was a bit like love, but discovery in art is like that, don't you think? When you hear Louis Armstrong sing "Saint James Infirmary" for the first time or Billie Holliday sing "Strange Fruit" or Dawn Upshaw sing the opening lines of the James Agee–Samuel Barber "Knoxville: Summer, 1915": "It has become that time of evening when people sit on their porches, rocking gently and talking gently and watching the street and the standing up into their sphere of possession of the trees." I thought, *How can I love this without being crushed by it?*

I was helped along in college by a close friend, a young composer, who would play things for me, and I for him, which furthered my musical education. We both loved Sondheim, and he has since scored for him, and I remember one night staying at his flat on the Upper West Side during a thunderstorm and listening to a recording of Sir Edward Elgar's *Sea Pictures*, sung by Kathleen Ferrier, as the lightning flashed in the dark. He really turned me on to Mahler, and I think I may have thrown a few light switches for him but couldn't say about what.

I found Janet Baker's recording of *Sea Pictures* and then her recordings of Schubert, Strauss, Fauré, and Britten, and I was really gone. She was so strong she could almost break, so steady she could sound like the end of the world were near. Her poise, so English, seemed to actually make so many emotional colors possible. And there always seemed an inbred note of sorrow that was completely authentic in her color.

I bought a ticket and went to Carnegie Hall by myself, which, even though I had grown up going to many of New York's great cultural institutions and had been to Carnegie Hall before for pop concerts and to see Groucho

Marx give his valedictory concert, these had all been what we might, just for shorthand, call middlebrow evenings. Even expensive theater tickets were a prerogative of the bourgeoisie. But there was a cultural divide for classical music when I was growing up, and there still is. My father may have scrounged twenty cents together to go hear Lawrence Tibbett or Ezio Pinza or Zinka Milanov, but no one I knew outside of the expensive liberal arts college I attended had ever been to Alice Tully Hall or the Met or to Carnegie Hall for the philharmonic. The Romantic era of proletarian classical music adoration and opera love wasn't untrue, but it was, I think, fleeting. I'm sure there must have been enculturated pockets of opera and symphony lovers in the neighborhoods of Brooklyn or Queens when I was growing up in New York, but the world of classical music performance was a black hole to me. The opera was something rich people went to—weren't they all in tuxes and gowns in the performances that flashed across the screen occasionally on PBS? The dress code was another form of not-too-subtle social exclusion. I associated tuxes with weddings, bar mitzvahs, and the Marx Brothers.

So, while Carnegie Hall wasn't entirely new to me, this version of it, for a performance of lieder, was. I had been raised, though, to generally be able to fake my way in any cultural milieu in which I was uncomfortable. Part of the reason for this was that despite having grown up in a modest row house in a working-class neighborhood, my father's travel agency allowed him to take us all around the world. And I was given a great sampling of manners and customs. But faking it was also part of our métier, part of the household training, our regimen and requirement. My father endlessly told the story of his first cruise, in 1933, while working for a travel business and how he was just lost at how to sit and eat at table, until it dawned on him that all he need do was delay his responses and imitate, order what the person next to him had ordered and eat the way they ate. It was this assimilationist strategy, already in the air in our general cultural class of first- and second-generation Jews, that fed much of what we did. We would all talk in various accents. We would travel under pseudonyms. And we would sing songs in keys and registers completely foreign to our home key, if in fact we knew what that was. I didn't until I started studying voice in college.

The two songs I've sung the most over the years have been "If I Only Had a Brain," the Yip Harburg–Harold Arlen composition from Wizard of Oz, and "The Way You Look Tonight," by Dorothy Fields and Jerome Kern. I've just realized that if you put them together you get a pretty hilarious title: "The Way You Look Tonight if I Only Had a Brain." It sounds like the theme song for the *Bride of Frankenstein*. I think there are emotional and musical reasons for the dominance of these two songs in my psychical and neurological playlist. With each I have spent years perseverating phrases, singing parts of the song internally or frequently out loud, walking down the street, walking into a classroom (my students have looked sometimes amused, sometimes bemused, hearing me, yet again, quietly singing, "With the thoughts I'd be thinkin' I could be another Lincoln if I only had a brain" as I set my books down on my desk), or cooking dinner.

I sing constantly, and in fact I do sing with some variety. I especially sing while I walk. I *always* sing while I walk. I might be singing something from *The Threepenny Opera* or a Dory Previn song or something by the Pogues. But more often than not, I'll be singing something from Tin Pan Alley or the Brill Building, and usually it will be a song I encountered before the age of eighteen. Of course that's a very large repertoire, but early music is like anything early: the deep grooves of engrams stretch as far into the future as we can see, think, or sing.

Nevertheless, these two songs have dominated, and I have a vague sense of why I repeat them somewhere on the continuum of mania, mantra, and novena. *The Wizard of Oz* is my favorite film, showing up in bits and pieces in much of what I've written. I think from the earliest age I responded most to a sense of deep estrangement in the film that no tidy ending was ever able to cure. The sense of not being taken care of in a hostile world and then having to take care of yourself in a strange world was a binary that bore into me. Surrounding the psychological whirlpool of the film were, and are, its deep pleasures: musical, cinematic, vaudevillian, all of which I had grown up with and went straight into my veins. The song "If I Only Had a Brain," coming as it does around midway in the film, is *very* catchy, and as with jingles, the easy and insistent musical and lyrical repetitions make it more liable to *stick*. "If I Only Had a Brain" (with its cohorts, heart and *da nerve*) is really a lament but, like one of the Child Ballads, a lament tricked out in singsong patter. That tricking of the emotional register hooked me early. I repeat it, I know, when the sorrows of the moment, the day, the year, the life, are looming, as they too often do for me, alas, child of anxiety as I am. I have responsibilities, though, and a sense of social decorum—a child, students, the desire to not look too mad on the street, which means that I'm not able or liable to yield to the pressures I generally feel to just sit down in my metaphorical cornfield and point both ways. So, I sing this little bit of song . . . *if I only had a brain . . . oh, I could tell you why* . . . as a way of trying to keep the lament, the pressure to be up and about and on the brick road, in check. Does it work? As Beckett writes in *Happy Days*, "Sorrow keeps breaking in." So, what is one to do? For now this bit of perseveration, as many years as it's lasted, seems to have helped a bit to keep away Elmira Gulch, whom, I suspect, is actually the world. And I keep moving, keep singing, to quote Mark Strand, "to keep things whole."

I love the story of the writing of "The Way You Look Tonight" by Jerome Kern and Dorothy Fields. They were working on *Swing Time*, one of the greatest Astaire-Rogers musicals (directed by George Stevens), and Kern had come up with the melody first. Fields writes: "The first time Jerry [Kern] played that melody for me I went out and started to cry. The release absolutely killed me. I couldn't stop, it was so beautiful." I'm not exactly sure what she means by the "release," though I like the way it sounds, its emotional valence. I think she's more or less talking about the bridge, the transition that occurs after the second verse, for which she wrote:

With each word your tenderness grows
Tearing my fear apart
And that laugh, that wrinkles your nose
It touches my foolish heart.

Why did it so move her—the story itself is moving—and why does it so move us? I think it's because the song, recorded by so many, begins with a melancholy note, projecting ahead to a time when the lovers will be parted, trying to find solace in the oncoming loss with the possession of love in the moment. The song, as much as Andrew Marvell's "To His Coy Mistress," is about time ("never ever change") and trying to figure out what to do, say, and feel about its ravages.

The brilliance of "The Way You Look Tonight" is the perfect balance of its tensions. "When the world is cold" indeed: someday, as the song's beginning suggests, the world itself will not just be cold to us but will be cold finally. But can we be happy knowing that tonight her "warm" smile is warm enough? For me the clinching line has always been "There is nothing for me but to love you." As idiosyncratic diction, the singer is saying he has no choice but to love and also that nothing else exists in the world with the same existential appeal and allure. We hear "There is nothing for me but," and we also manage to hear, "There is nothing for me." He's tender, yes, but there's sophisticated desperation in the heart of this song.

And the release. Or the bridge. The two words together form a troubling suggestion. As the music surges, his mistress "tears his fear apart" ("like amorous birds of prey"?), sets her apart from him as a creature living in the moment. For the last stanza the singer only has poignancy left. He repeats that his beloved is "lovely," a lovely word no doubt if not quite an immortal adjective, and implores her as a child would to "never never change" and keep her "breathless charm." Need I comment? *The grave's a fine and private . . .* And asking her to "arrange it" glibly, he finally says: "'Cause I love you / Just the way you look tonight." Repeat. Our sense at song's end is that the night is almost over, time hasn't been vanquished; memory, time's handmaiden, is waiting at the door.

Supposedly, Kern's melody borrows, in changed key, from "Lang, lang währt der sommer nicht," a duet from Emmerich Kálmán's operetta *Der Zigeunerprimas*. It walks a kind of melodic tightrope between major and minor keys. And Fields's emotional response to the first hearing translated into one of the great melancholy love songs, plagued by time. The only song I can think of that even approaches its effect is the Beatles's "Things We Said Today," a minor key masterpiece that also looks ahead and then back.

I sing "The Way You Look Tonight," which I'm sure I first heard as a young child watching and rewatching Astaire-Rogers films on TV in Brooklyn, no doubt to an invented other, imagining an invented night of looming loss. I'm sure the music hooked me—Kern after all was one of the two or three greatest popular composers of Tin Pan Alley—and it may make little sense to try to separate music and lyrics, though I've often felt a special affinity with Dorothy Fields over the years, perhaps because her lyrics feel a bit different to me, strange, intense. I sing this song over and over to myself, trying, I think, to make the transition in the *release* so that it sounds passable as a way of continuing, year after year, to console myself for the failure to find that partner to successfully bond with over time. Oh, marriage, relationships, yes, yes. They've come and gone. But still . . . the world is cold. And one way of keeping the cold world from cracking is by singing about it, by singing a song about how I, he, the singer, was bound to be here, years later, thinking back on that night. It's a, shall we say, *cold* comfort in many ways. But as I've perseverated this lovely ballad over the decades, my fears, such as they still continue to be, at least have a beautiful melody. And one stays in the song, the same song one has been singing for decades, which is a prop, a sop, a crutch . . . an offering to Cupid, to perhaps lay off.

Oliver Sacks died two days ago, the day after I had begun reading his book *Musicophilia* with an eye, or an ear, toward this essay. And today Dean Jones died. That may sound like an unlikely combination of dead-fellows, the brilliant writer-neurologist and the man known mostly for Disney films like *Herbie*. But I had a very personal connection to both men, having interviewed Sacks many years ago and having brought him to Ohio University, where I was teaching. He also gave me a brilliant essay on memory for an anthology I edited. And we kept up fitfully. I had an intensely personal musical connection with Dean Jones—if only at a distance, however—forged when I was fourteen.

Jones had taken a leave from his string of Disney roles (*Herbie, The Love Bug*) to star in *Company*, Stephen Sondheim's groundbreaking musical, in

1970. Jones had the lead role of Bobby, the man who, while attracted to his friends' wives, couldn't make a commitment to any one woman. He imagines taking the best parts of each of these women in "Someone Is Waiting," creating his ideal, a Frankensteinish romantic idyll:

A Susan sort of Sarah,
A Jennyish Joanne . . .
Wait for me, I'm ready now
I'll find you if I can.

His magnum opus in *Company,* and Sondheim's favorite of his songs, is *Being Alive.* Sung on Bobby's fortieth birthday, it's an intense performance, taken almost to the breaking point. (It was captured vividly on the DVD of the making of the cast recording, which Jones had been invited to record even though he had dropped out of *Company* after several weeks because, supposedly, it was all too close to home and his marriage was suffering). The song begins with a catalog of what the trouble with having a loved other is:

Someone to hold you too close,
Someone to hurt you too deep,
Someone to sit in your chair,
To ruin your sleep.

The song continues the catalog of love's misbegotten labors, its demands, deepening the singer's sense of panic that he's been avoiding a crowning experience of intimacy:

Someone to crowd you with love,
Someone to force you to care,
Someone to make you come through,
Who'll always be there,
As frightened as you
Of being alive.

The realization transforms him, and blowing out his candles, the pronoun changes from *someone* to *somebody*; a catalog of indignation changes into a wish, a prayer: "Somebody hold me too close."

Dean Jones's version of "Being Alive" made an indelible impression on me when I saw it at age thirteen. That song, those songs in *Company*, were crucial to my sense of independent thinking, my faith in my own critical reactions. My family was confused by how new the music and staging of *Company* was, but I furiously defended it and articulated it. It was the first time in my life I felt with complete certainty that my critical appraisal was the *necessary* way of seeing something, always a bit of a mirage, but so, well, necessary to anyone whose life is largely going to be based on the forming and defending of opinions, on aesthetic judgments and distinctions. "Being Alive" has been recorded by several other singers, but none have the sense of dramatic progress or feel as much is at stake (everything?) as in Dean Jones's version.

I've sung "Being Alive" many times over the years but never for an audience. It's very hard to sing (it ranges through octaves like "The Star Spangled Banner"), and the repetitions of *being alive* at the end require so much vocal range that I end up sounding like I'm about to burst my goiter when I sing it, like a caricature of someone singing way out of their range. I sound like I should be rushed to a hospital. But I *do* sing it to myself, as I do many Stephen Sondheim songs, mostly from the extraordinary period of 1970–81 (*Company, Follies, A Little Night Music, Pacific Overtures, Sweeny Todd, Merrily We Roll Along*—which I just realized is the entire Hal Prince period). It's the song I sing over the years when my sense of intimacy is perilous, threatened, or thin. There is the actually singing we do, whether at full volume or sotto voce walking through a crowd. But we also do a kind of silent singing, not a listening but singing, in our voices, in our head. Many times I've sung "Being Alive" at just the right pitch, the right register, and fully in my own voice. This lyrical ventriloquism, throwing our voices inside ourselves, as though it were a special frequency—you know, AM, FM, and, what, IM?—seems to me central to what I've heard through the years or what I've needed to hear: myself giving voice to important songs that I couldn't sing well or couldn't sing in the moment (people in airplanes really will think you're crazy if you start doing both parts of "If I Loved You"). When I'm awfully low, I need to sing whether or not any sound is produced.

In any case I began this digression with news of two deaths and end with "Being Alive." "Being Alive" is being human and vulnerable, and this, of course, would be impossible without our sense of the carnage that life also has in store for us. I can't imagine not singing through that. It's a self-soothing mechanism.

I never participated in any organized singing, any chorus of any kind, in high school; my voice then was really devoted to politics, to the remnants of the Vietnam War and my undying enmity for Richard Nixon. Almost everyone who wrote in my high school yearbook said something about impeaching Nixon. The singing I was doing, alone in my room, tended to be either the impassioned singer-songwriter material having its heyday: Dylan, Simon and Garfunkel, Joni Mitchell, Cat Stevens, but I also went deep into the folk canon for political singers who seemed attuned to what I was feeling in my youthful, politically passionate heart: Woody Guthrie, Big Bill Broonzy, Ewan MacColl, and Peggy Seeger, assorted songs of the labor movement that I still sing all the time: "Which Side Are You On?" which I sing when I want to summon the outrage of disinvolvement ("They say in Harlan County / there are no neutrals there / You'd better be a union man / or a thug for J. H. Blair") or "Sit Down" or Joe Hill's "The Preacher and the Slave" ("Work and pray, live on hay / You'll get pie in the sky when you die"). As they were and are supposed to, these songs *activated* me, kept me emotionally engaged with the struggles of the Left that I was a little neophyte in. That's what their classic purpose has been. Songs have always, after all, served a social and political function, whether they were the emotional and cultural center of family life before media and general literacy. People sang and told stories, but frequently they told stories by singing. And they sang when they worked, so they didn't work too hard. We mostly listen these days, I think.

It dawned on me, when I went to college, that having this instrument that I carted around from place to place . . . it might be nice to develop it a little, to see what it was capable of. So, I signed up for voice class and ended up taking lessons, individual, small and large group, for a year and a half. This was one of those almost arbitrary decisions one makes when one is eighteen that reverberates throughout life. Taking voice completely changed my relationship to singing, to the production of sound. I studied under a man who had a cultlike following at my little liberal arts college. Usually, this would have made me run for the hills. I then, and still do, shy away from personality cults. I've always thought charisma should be used for charming the person sitting next to you, rather than having a group think you're infallible. Really, though, who wanted to be another *comer* for the attention of an ego-fed DemiProf. Oh, well, there wasn't much choice, and the professor in question was just returning, rather enfeebled, from a stroke. Well, he was supposed to be a special teacher.

Frank, even in his paper-whispery reduced state, semi-paralyzed, was rather good to work with. True, I had to fend off his wandering hands when, in showing me how to sing from the diagram, he too frequently missed and shot lower, but a pseudo-stern upbraiding would correct the fault temporarily. Learning not to squeeze sound from your throat is a wonderful thing. Learning to let air push up through you and make reasonably pleasant sounds is a charming way to like your body better, something I was always on the lookout for. And then to be told, on occasion, "You sing well," that the sounds you produce actually are pleasing to another, has always thrilled me. I would rather be told I sing well than these things:

Drive well
Cook well
Make sense in an argument
Tell a funny story
Predict the weather with reasonable accuracy
Perform various sexual functions that involve costumes
Serve as a host
Behave as a guest, etc.

You get the point, I think. By the way, I'm not quite sure of one of the items on the list. But to be told I sing well means to me that my listener and I are receiving pleasure from David as an *instrument*. I'm a kind of clarinet or an oboe for those moments—I'm playing myself, and some delight is available. And it is delightful to delight.

The audience who has most heard my voice is my son. Perhaps he feels he has heard it too much. I imagine I was the first person whom he heard sing, as I sang to him almost immediately. The spigot has been flowing constantly since. I have lived longer and more closely with him than with any other person, if you except my own birth family, and the bond between us is equally intense and familiar, easier than any other, and properly warier at times than many. I've sung him many of the songs I've mentioned in this essay since his infancy and many others too. He has outdone me in his knowledge of Spike Jones since I started singing and then playing those songs for him when he was a toddler; he gobbled them up and made them part of his inner songscape.

One winter day, when I was feeling especially low, about two years ago, he beckoned me upstairs to our Loft, where he was on his keyboard. "Listen," he said. He had taught himself the melody of "The Way You Look Tonight," perfect pitchmeister that he is, having heard me sing it ten thousand times, as a way of trying to please me, to cheer me up. Like Dorothy Fields on her first flight into the melody with Jerome Kern, I burst into tears.

Delmore, my son, and I make up a lot of songs. Especially while walking. Sometimes they're ad hoc improvisations on melodies we know (amputator anyone?); sometimes I just invent a new song to see if he's really listening. I've done this for years.

Oh, the bitterest tears
When you're at the Graveyard Bar
And no one knows your reckless name
Flow like moldy sidecars.

He'll get a strange, quizzical look on his face and turn to me and say, "Is that a real song?" "No," I'll say, "what's the next verse?" And he'll provide it.

That run into the sea
Because they've lost their handlebars.

So, do we do homage to the tradition of song, of homely household song-writing, all of which vanishes almost immediately. Sometimes he'll like one and say, "You should write it down," but that would be antagonistic to the spirit of the thing for me.

The first song I remember singing as a child, which I have written of elsewhere: "My Bonnie Lies over the Ocean." I loved singing this because it both soothed me and gave me a pang of melancholy at the same time. I think this is still true of many of the songs I sing. Robert Burton, in *The Anatomy of Melancholy*, suggests that song can cure or deepen melancholy but that sometimes "it is a pleasing melancholy that it causeth; and therefore to such as are discontent, in woe, fear, sorrow, or dejected, it is a most present remedy." Singing has often been this for me. "My Body Lies over the Ocean," I heard, and it was both saddening and somehow pleasing to think of the body so far away but that one could sing it back: Bring back, bring back, bring back my body . . . I think I'm still trying to bring it back, to sing it back, a kind of anti-Siren or muse to my own self.

So, if you pass me on the street, walking down Broadway in Chicago, perhaps, or going for an aimless stroll down Hudson Street, if I'm back in New York, and I look animated, perhaps even a bit tearful, from fifteen or twenty feet away, don't be alarmed when you pass me and instead of conversational Bluetooth, you hear something like actual melody escaping from my lips. When I was a boy, my mother told me that she sang to make herself cry. I didn't understand that at all as an adolescent—I didn't want to, since that was the adolescent emotional métier. Why would you want to make yourself cry? Of course, I understand now. Nevertheless, considerably older than my own mother was ever to live, I'm usually singing for quite a different purpose: not to.

LOLLIPOP
IS MINE

I had an epiphany near the Carrier Corporation in Syracuse on a wicked cold day. I realize how inauspicious this sounds, but we take them when we can get them, right? And quite frankly, I'm more apt to trust mud puddle realizations than I am any grand information about the meaning of life that comes to me while gazing out at an Umbrian vista drinking a glass of wine. Don't get me wrong (or alternately, get me wrong, which might in itself prove interesting), I'm not advocating dreariness or suggesting that the only way to know life in some authentic way is through, well, anything. I think that's the point. I'm too old for formulas. I'm just saying that disjunction at least has some innate friction in it that can make life interesting.

Anyhow, as I was saying, I was by the Carrier Corporation, and it was cold, as it is apt to be in Syracuse in the winter. I was there as a graduate student, over thirty years ago now, studying creative writing, with wonderful teachers like Ray Carver and Philip Booth and my mentor in poetry, Hayden Carruth. I was working on my thesis, a long fractured series of poetic dramatic monologues linked by narrative, based on the life of the folksinger Phil Ochs. I think in some ways I was trying to write out my obsession with Phil Ochs, whose music I had been listening to over and over for years. I suffer from a kind of musical hyper-perseveration, and I'm apt to listen to and sing the same songs (not necessarily to the exclusion of others but with an alarming regularity) repeatedly, for months or years. And it was the songs' twining with Phil Ochs life and fate—his life as protest singer and activist, then mournful autobiographical lyricist, then crazy street persona and sad washout, culminating with his suicide at his sister's house on Long Island, in 1976, at the age of thirty-six—that haunted me and kept me hooked into the world of his work. I remember where I was when I heard that he had killed himself, in my library carrel at Bennington College, which tells you something. I remember where I was for the deaths of four other famous people: Nat King Cole, Adlai Stevenson, Fred Astaire, and John Lennon. Make of that what you will.

Hayden Carruth, my professor, who was an extraordinary poet and critic of jazz, was curious about the music, so I'd sit in his office, playing him tapes of Ochs singing, his early stuff, "There but for Fortune" or "Santo Domingo," and his late semi-suicidal songs, "The Scorpion Departs but Never Returns" or "William Butler Yeats Visits Lincoln Park and Escapes Unscathed." Hayden really liked them, as I recall, and he didn't like much.

I know I started by telling you that I was going to write about an epiphany, and I will. And it actually is about music but music of a very different kind. But there's a reason I was listening to it, and that had much to do with Phil Ochs.

I've always been pleased that I managed to see Ochs live twice—once when he organized the Concert for Allende, after Salvador Allende was overthrown, in 1975. This was at the Felt Forum in New York, and Ochs had his famous reunion with Bob Dylan onstage, which was more like the two of them merely being on the same stage. For those of you, I imagine a rather significant portion of my readership, who are not up on the private vendettas of singers from the sixties, supposedly Dylan asked Ochs what he thought of a song, and Ochs said he didn't think much of it, and Dylan threw him out of his limousine, this around 1966. Some people thought Dylan wrote "Positively 4th Street" about Ochs, but that never made much sense to me.

I also saw Ochs in 1974, when he organized the War Is Over concert in Central Park. I remember mostly that Joan Baez and Paul Simon were there and that there weren't as many people there as I would have thought. They sang Ochs's song "The War Is Over." Perhaps it's hard to get as many people to show up for a celebration of something finally ending, especially when it seemed to end with a whimper.

I have to shift scenes here, to California, in 1978, when I looked like a more angelic Roger Daltrey or less kinky Kinky Friedman and was going to graduate school, though when I think back on it, I marvel that just a couple of years earlier, I was sleeping in my basement bedroom in Brooklyn . . . Those are wildly intense years, fifteen to twenty-one, I think, as our songs struggle out of the lower echelons. We go from having our lunches packed for us to, well, a whole lot of trouble and bliss.

For some reason, in California I started listening to doo-wop all the time. I started buying doo-wop albums, collections on Laurie but also obscure stuff on Holiday and Crimson and Beltone. I still have these albums. Why did I start listening to doo-wop fifteen years after its prime—and yikes, that doesn't sound like so much from this distance, when doo-wop seems like ancient history, and from the geographical remove of its birthplaces on the East Coast? It's amusing to wonder who I was, driving three thousand miles by myself, listening to Ralph Vaughn Williams in Kansas at sunset or Joni Mitchell as I was pitching through the Rockies, anxious to get myself to my new home and the perception that on a new coast I would find all of these new contours of a new self. I wasn't entirely wrong.

But to get back to music, I'm not exactly sure what, at that stage of my development, when I was branching out into all kinds of jazz and classical music, led me into an obsession with doo-wop, unless it was a subconscious association of it with my childhood and New York. I mean, Dion was practically a saint in my neighborhood in Brooklyn, and I have and had dim memories of guys riding around in cars when I was a tike and throwing bits of the Belmonts and the Four Seasons out the windows on warm summer days and nights: "I should have known it from the very start" and "I'll tell the world forget about it girl." Doo-wop was primarily African American and Italian American in practice; maybe in Northern California, which seemed very white and suburban to me in the late seventies, I was needing a little "neighborhood" playing in the background.

I started listening to doo-wop all the time, but I didn't really know it, other than the obvious "hits" one would hear in passing from the radio stations, from oldies shows. And even most of these weren't songs that registered that deeply in me. Oldies were so old in the seventies. Doo-wop in all its permutations made its way onto my playlist—the early groups like the Penguins, the great Italian American groups like the Belmonts, the Mystics and Randy and the Rainbows. And brilliant black groups like Frankie Lymon and the Teenagers, the Coasters and the Platters. Lyrically, doo-wop generally captured a pretty primal, young experience, but then again, I was really young and reasonably primal myself, having found what felt like some kind of loophole to get myself away from the Naked City and the naked self. I wanted to clothe myself in California in a cooler, more ironic persona. But that also meant I had developed an absolute need to hear the Marcels sing "Blue Moon," the Rodgers and Hart standard I knew too well, and with Hoagy Carmichael's "Heart and Soul" one of the templates for the kind of chord progression and standards revisionism that doo-wop would embody.

One of the crucial elements of many doo-wop songs (this isn't the epiphany) is the division of lead between a classic tenor and a falsetto (or a falsetto and a bass), sometimes sung by the same singer, as in the case with Frankie Valli and Dion, or sometimes split between singers, as with the Del-Vikings (a group that was integrated—important and unusual for the time, 1955). But I loved this division, or split, as though the single voice weren't quite enough so that the consciousness of the song needed to expand its sense of persona to have a more lyrical voice or a slightly gritty and lyrical sensibility, representing both sides of what is invariably a lover's sensibility. But there is a very practical sense in which a different mode of articulation needed to be available, a formal shift to emphasize intensification, which was represented by the falsetto. Writers sometimes do this with typography, shifting into italics, breaking prose with verse, etc.

Doo-wop has its sillier side, novelty songs like "The Lion Sleeps Tonight" by the Tokens, which is still fun to listen to, or "Oh, My Mother-in-Law" by the Volumes or "Rubber Biscuit" by the Chips. You don't have to look far, but doo-wop's attempt to sing something in a new way frequently still feels very fresh and charming.

Before I stop my general disquisition on doo-wop, on this medium-length foray into a story of musical epiphany, I must mention "Moulty" by the Barbarians. Frequently included in doo-wop anthologies, it's a late addition and represents some of the qualities of classic doo-wop, notably a spoken narrative, though it also points to garage music and the creeping British Invasion. Doo-wop, and the Girl Groups, which are an extension and development of doo-wop, really pushed spoken narrative as a motif, in songs like "Remember (Walking in the Sand)" by the Shangri-Las, "My Boyfriend's Back" by the Angels, "Leader of the Pack" also by the Shangri-Las, "Do You Love Me" by the Contours, and "Little Darlin'" by the Diamonds.

I created a small cult around the song when I was a graduate student at Syracuse, always playing it at parties. The song begins with the nerdy-sounding voice of a man, the voice *sounding* like Buddy Holly *looks*, accompanied by a melancholy harmonica:

I remember the days when
Things were real bad for me
It was right after my accident
When I lost my hand.

There's a great accident motif in doo-wop—a classic way for lovers to separate—except in Moulty the speaker has been separated from his hand. It turns out he's the drummer of the band. The song tells us that he was very depressed as the rest of the band's refrain keeps kicking in: "Moulty!" (apparently the singer's name).

Don't turn away (you gotta, baby)
Don't turn away (you gotta keep on trying)
Don't turn away, don't turn away.

The high point of the song, the turning point, the verse that makes the one-armed drummer decide to embrace the world and keep on living is:

Now there's just one thing that I need
Not sympathy and I don't want no pity
But a girl, a real girl
One that really loves me
And then I'll be the complete man.

How can I tell you how much we loved the lyric, "a real girl . . . And then I'll be the complete man"? Poor Moulty. How we laughed at your expense. We did say silent prayers that you were able to move on to a "real girl," though we always thought you were a complete man, as much as that is a thing to be desired. Some absurdities can simply never be exhausted. Think of Spike Jones.

I also have to say a word about "I Love You" by the Volumes, and this in fact might serve as a kind of introduction to the epiphany that you may have forgotten that you're waiting for. I certainly haven't, though I worry that you're going to want a really good one, like that high note that Frankie Valli would pull out at the end of a song.

"I Love You" is not a promising title for a song. My reason is, well, it's the shadow title for every song ever written. The lyrics to the song are beyond disposable. They could have been written in two minutes on a napkin, but they should have stayed there. Yet that's part of the song's power, the fact that the lead singer, the tenor, who sounds young and slightly rough around the edges, is trying to articulate his feelings. This is really one of my favorite lead vocals because he actually sounds like everyone's inner teenager trying to find the words. He really can't find words that are incredibly new ("Your love is oh so heavenly / My darling can't you see") which is why he ends up repeating "I love you" over and over again, along with "I need you." But he's a teenager in love, and the strength of his feeling, the yearning he sings with, lets us know that finding language for feeling is just so difficult. But we have the music of his singing and his attempt, which leads to what is for me one of the, if not the, most ethereally beautiful moments in doo-wop and in pop music: after the second verse the falsetto lead, with doo-wop reverb and echo, sings, "Doo-doo-doo-doo-do-do, do-do-do-do-do-do-do-do, doo-ooh-ooh-ooh-ooh," which is haunting and ethereal, as though the singer had just entered a magical world, as though the voice had just become suddenly a kind of even mystical joy, followed by his tenor "I love yous." It captures a joyous love rapture better than anything I know. I used it at my wedding. I guess that means I can't use it again, were I ever . . . That would be crass. Alas.

That really should have been the epiphany, shouldn't it? But I'm going to return to Syracuse, which sounds like Plautus via Rodgers and Hart. I was driving by the plant of the Carrier Corporation in 1981, a couple of years after I had left California, left my little golden sojourn with its doo-wop soundtrack, and here I was back east, in the Rust Belt, driving by the plant of the largest company in town, I don't remember why, at the end of the day, with lots of men walking, walking toward their cars, looking tired, but there was a marvelous cold bright sunset coming on, this being middle fall, a kind of orange glow in the sky silhouetting all of these tired men, and I remember—I'm sure you've had moments like this—feeling a kind of sympathy for them, though not sentimentally, precisely what Hazlitt called (and claimed to have coined) "disinterested," meaning not a lack of interest but the absence of a personal or autobiographical stake or claim but certainly not an absence of keen or astute interest in the nature of well-being of these people; just the opposite, I felt an enormous, sharp sympathy that was merely human.

It was at this moment that the station I had tuned in, an oldies station, started playing the song "Lollipop" by the Chordettes. "Lollipop" was written by Beverly Ross and Julius Dixon in 1957, auspiciously the year of my birth, though unconnected to it, apparently after Dixon's daughter had gotten a lollipop stuck in her hair, inspiring Dixon on a consonantal binge as she repeated the word over and over again, and Dixon wrote the melody on the spot. Ross and a neighbor boy recorded a demo of the song as Ronald and Ruby, and it charted, though not at the level the white girl group the Chordettes would attain a year later. I actually quite like the early version of the song by Ronald and Ruby. It's more stripped-down, a bit less varnished, than the next year's megahit. It has the slightly raw quality of some of my favorite doo-wop songs. But they only play the Chordettes's version on the radio.

The Chordettes weren't properly a doo-wop group, but the song they produced with "Lollipop," complete with added-on and uncredited bass intoning *da-dum-dum-dum*, followed by the popping of a cheek, certainly sounds like doo-wop by any standards—close echoey harmony, teen love, bass counterpoint to the sopranos, etc. Like "I Love You," the song is mostly in the melody and the singing, since the lyrics, while amusing, aren't exactly Chekhovian in their complexity:

Sweeter than candy on a stick
Huckleberry, cherry, or lime
If you had a choice he'd be your pick
But Lollipop is mine.

Lollipop Lollipop
Oh Lolli Lolli Lolli Lollipop Lollipop
Oh Lolli Lolli Lolli Lollipop Lollipop
Oh Lolli Lolli Lolli Lollipop *POP*

Crazy way he thrills me
Tell you why
Just like a lightning from the sky
He loves to kiss me till I can't see straight
Gee, my Lollipop is great!

I call him . . .

Well, I told you. And I suppose one could go as far as to say that the song is a precursor of "bubblegum" music, that much maligned phenomenon of the mid- to late sixties to early seventies that substituted saccharine for sugar in the pop music of the era. Think "Sugar, Sugar," quite the misnomer, by the Archies. However, "Lollipop," and just barely mind you, still has the benefit of sounding actually teenaged, the yearning semi-authentic, and the young women's harmonies blending in and out to create a soundscape that catches you by surprise with its intensity. The track has a heavy rhythm section, bass and drums, which provides a sense of contrast to the chorus sound of the women. And the women are layered in two tracks on the first refrain, both singing the lyrics and also singing, wordlessly, in harmony at the same time. The song ends with a cappella singing. So, there's a lot going on in two minutes and ten seconds, which is one of the things that lovers of pop music always embrace.

So, as I said at the top, I was driving by the Carrier Corporation on this fall afternoon, and "Lollipop" came on the radio, the song introduced casually by claps at the beginning. I turned it up. When the girls hit the refrain, I tell you now, unashamedly, I started weeping. I thought it was so ethereal, like I was Rip Van Winkle and had woken up to "Clair de Lune"—the sound felt new, and the effect was transporting. That's what mattered most. And the thought that came into my mind was that popular music was sacred music, that "Lollipop" was just "Ave Maria" with a bandwidth.

And that thought on that day thrilled me, that a bunch of teenaged girls singing about Lollipop were no different than the Tallis Scholars or the Anonymous 4 or the Collegium Vocale Ghent, with groups of singers releasing Monteverdi's or Bach's madrigals or cantatas, their choral texts about God or wounded love, to exquisite depth.

That was my epiphany, that afternoon thirty-five years and several digressions ago. Since then, I've never made excuses for anything I loved listening to or watching, as long as it rose to the level of "Lollipop."

BRUSHES WITH THE GREAT
AND NOT-SO-GREAT

We talk about the excessive veneration of celebrity in our culture with well-honed disgust; we even have celebrities who are mostly famous for their love of, following of, emulation of, and writing about celebrities. We have celebrities who are celebrities for their mockery of celebrities. They become minor satellites in the universe of stardom, unlike those who, in the words of Lina Lamont in *Singin' in the Rain*, become "a shimmering, glowing star in the cinema firmament." She then adds, "It says so right here." Celebrity needs confirmation, affirmation. And so, no matter how blasé we tend to be about those whose star shines brighter than our own, we tend to move closer to it when it appears. "Hey, it's Hulk Hogan!" And we rush to get a gander because said large, doltish man has appeared before so many millions of us. He has, therefore, by the logic of the magic of the masses and the image, some kind of Benjaminian aura. Children are especially susceptible to the draw of celebrities. In the same way that they think everything written on the Internet is true, they think anyone who has ever been in a movie has talent, and as a child, I pursued autographs of celebrities with an at times alarming celerity.

After my mother had died, I learned that she had tossed my beloved autograph album out (Buzz Aldrin, Martin Balsam, Steve Lawrence and Eydie Gorme, Bella Abzug . . .). The great and almost great, or not so great, sat side by side in happy incongruity until their casual dissolution. When I found out the album was gone, I felt a pang of anger at my dead mother: all those years of chasing down the perceived glitter of immortality, just vanished. But it's so hard to stay mad at the dead. Believe me, I've tried: they have a kind of quiet insouciance that always manages to disarm.

One of my earliest memories is of walking up Fifth Avenue with my father, holding his hand and walking north. It's a reasonably balmy memory. Some memories come with weather; some do not. Most of the weather in memory is stock from studio films anyway. The lightning flashes bright. The thunder is a drumroll. It's a flashy kind of effect, since the weather of our lives is mostly undramatic. Unless the weather, that is, is the center of the memory itself. But that's not the case on this day. We're walking near Saks Fifth Avenue, and my father says, to no one in particular, "Look who's here," or something like that. I'm about five years old, and we walk up to a talk man in a sweater. I remember the sweater more than the man. The man says, "Leo, how are you doing?" My father says, "Pretty good, Perry. This is my kid, David." Or something like that. They shake hands. I shake his hand. They chat. And we move on. My father tells me that this was Perry Como, a very big television star. My father is always acquiring aura in this way. Sure, he knows a really big TV star. Sure, he knows a really big movie star. But will touching the hand of the famous man, the man who makes my father famous by a degree of separation, make me less likely to fill with anxiety when I have done something wrong and my father lifts the receiver and threatens to give me to the Gypsies? I'll give you two guesses. If your answer is wrong, I'm going to give you to the Kardashians.

For years my family had box seats for the Knicks behind the team's president, Ned Irish, at center court. Irish, one of the founders of the NBA, was pretty old by then—this was roughly, the late 1960s through the 1990s. Irish always looked unhappy. Even during the glory years, of Frazier and Reed, Bradley and DeBusschere, some of the best basketball you could imagine seeing played, Irish looked unhappy. My guess is he was just unhappy, but this is just a wild stab on my part. He was always there with his wife, who was French, and his wife's friend, also French. They seemed far from unhappy, perhaps because De Gaulle was *there*, and they were *here*. We had Nixon, but perhaps they weren't citizens and didn't have to care about anything except basketball. What I liked best about them, in addition to their matching beehive hairdos, was that when the Knicks were hunkering down trying to keep the opposition from scoring, they would shout, in French, "Défense, défense!" as though they were urging on some kind of movable Maginot Line. Irish always looked slightly discomfited at their vocal enthusiasm. When he glanced at my brother and me, which was rare, he had a slight air of disdain that two such unimportant waifs were sitting so close to him. I'm sure we managed to get the seats through my father's aura.

I used to collect autographs and several times either embarrassed myself or was simply humiliated by the act of trying to get the signature of a very famous, temporarily famous, or sort of famous person. In the lobby of the King David Hotel in Jerusalem, I asked "Mr. Mostel" for his autograph. "It's 'Mr. Mostel,' he said. "Calling me 'Zero,' at your age. It's disrespectful." I tried to stammer out a response, to no avail. He did sign a stray piece of something or other. I managed to repeat the same experience with a lesser celebrity, Henry Morgan, in an airport. This must have been around 1965, and he was on a lot of quiz shows. I would be shocked now if most readers of this paragraph had even a dim clue about who Henry Morgan was. He was a celebrity. A pseudo-wit. A semi-raconteur. He has faded into the Mists of Asterisks. I clearly had some uncanny, circuslike ability to make people think I was saying their first names when I was addressing them formerly. I sometimes think of the riches and fame I myself could have developed, how I could have been the person in the airport upbraiding a small child for calling me "David" instead of "Mr. Lazar," if the faculty I had of auditory transformation had been developed. This wan fantasy aside, Henry Morgan actually yelled at me, saying, "It's Mr. Morgan! Not 'Henry,'" with an enthusiasm that suggested he had been waiting for the opportunity to say those lines since he first donned a gray serge suit. He, though, would not sign an autograph because of my breach of apparent decorum. Instead, he sent me on my way as a few onlookers gawked—which is of course the prerogative of onlookers—and I made my desultory way back to my parents at the gate with only a story in my hands and a little heap of embarrassment to add to the sum I kept in reserve.

A nicer story is that I passed Dick Van Dyke on the street in New York once. This must have been in the mid-1970s. I shouted to him, rather genially, a version of a line from *The Dick Van Dyke Show*: "Hey, Rob, I've got dibs on Laura!" He smiled broadly and pointed at me. I smiled back. I'm assuming he heard me. He may have been smiling broadly and pointing at everyone back then.

One of my father's clients was Roy Cohn. Yes, *him*. My father was a travel agent who could book a ticket when no one else could, find a room when there were none available. He was really, really good. That's why he had a lot of celebrity clients. I met Cohn a couple of times. He was reasonably nice in that New York courtly way. There are variations of that style you get used to identifying if you grow up in New York. One version is rather patronizing. Cohn's leaned to that but not odiously. He was powerful but had taken his knocks, for excellent reasons. Another version of that type is quite gracious, of course, even solicitous. Nix that. In any case one day my father asked if I were interested at all in going to Studio 54. Studio 54 at the time was the hottest place in New York, almost impossible to get into. I said, "Well, yeah, sure. Uh-huh." I don't think my father knew about the blowjobs and the lines of coke. Of course, I stayed away from those myself. But when I was in New York, my father would phone Roy Cohn, who would leave my name at the door.

One time I was leaning against a pole, trying to figure out how I would sit next to Valerie Perrine again. I loved sitting next to Valerie Perrine. She was really friendly and would sort of rub up against you. I was on my second or fourth bourbon and spotted Divine, which was beyond exciting. It, it was... divine! I loved John Waters, and Divine was the embodiment of Watersworld, so beautifully gross and strange and feminine. I walked up to him and said,

"I just adore you, so would you please tell me, did you take your name from Genet?" and I wasn't trying to be precocious, but I loved *Our Lady of the Flowers* as much as I loved John Waters. Divine bent down and kissed me on the forehead. He had a half-devilish and half-sweet smile, and he said, "Aren't you a clever lad." He laughed good-naturedly and patted me on the cheek and walked away. And I was utterly elated.

The year I lived in London, 1985–86, was a banner year for brushes. I sat next to Michael Powell at the theater in London in 1985. When he came and sat down, I had one of those overwhelmingly heart-racing experiences: is it him, is it not? He was eighty by then, and I knew an earlier version of him. I finally convinced myself that it was Michael Powell because he sat and talked the way Michael Powell would. His asides and gestures seemed very knowingly directed. So, I said, "I don't mean to disturb you, Mr. Powell, but I'm a great fan of your films." "Very nice of you to say so, young man," he said. "Is there one in particular you like?" I told him that my particular favorite was *A Matter of Life and Death* (titled *Stairway to Heaven* in the United States). "Good choice." Twenty years later, after Powell died, I edited a book that covered interviews he had given in his career. But I don't remember if my meeting him had anything to do with the book or not, if that was or was not an incidental part in my coming to do that work. Some sequences, some parts of the influences on our lives, even reasonably significant ones, become untraceable at some point. Our memories are made up of so much white space.

Sometime that year I spotted Richard Thompson as I was waiting for a plane at Heathrow. He was hard to miss; he's about six foot everything. At the time I think was listening to three things, as I am sometimes wont to do (occasionally it's one or two): Richard Thompson's *Across a Crowded Room*, Loudon Wainwright's *I'm Alright*, and Tom Waits's *Rain Dogs*. I was completely under Thompson's sway. I had listened to his music beginning in the Fairport Convention days through his magical albums with Linda Thompson, and then his bitter solo albums seemed to yet still be reaching new places for bitter literary songwriting. *Across a Crowded Room*—his jaundiced invocation of Rodgers and Hammerstein's "Some Enchanted Evening"—is one of the most extraordinary albums I know, up there with albums like *Court and Spark* and *Who's Next*. It's a song suite on the perils of love set in Thatcher's England: "When the Spell Is Broken," "Love in a Faithless Country," "Fire in the Engine Room," "Walking through a Wasted Land." And, and . . . there Thompson was waiting, as I was, since the delays at Heathrow were horrendous. His persona in the last several albums he had done since the very public breakup of his marriage to Linda was so severe, so vituperative, that I was a little afraid of him. And he was really tall. But I wandered over and muttered something about how important I thought the new album was. Strangely, he grinned shyly and thanked me profusely. He seemed rather shy himself. And we then we both wandered away, shy flatterer and flatteree.

My trilogy of 1985 greats ends with what was at the time for me the greatest of all. In my teens I was a dyed-in-the-wool folk music junky (which is an entirely amusing combination to consider: banjo string wrapped around the arm, etc.). I got news that Peggy Seeger and Ewan MacColl were giving a concert in a room over a pub by the University of London and went down and grabbed a ticket post haste. It was strange then, and it's strange now: most people I knew and know have never heard of either of the two singer-songwriters, but they were legends for me. Peggy Seeger, the half-sister of Pete Seeger and twenty years MacColl's junior, had met and married him in the early 1950s. Both were radical; both were blacklisted in the United States because of Communist activities or affiliations. Their relationship was an additional scandal—MacColl was married to his second wife, with two young children with her, including the young Kirsty MacColl—but he left and soon wrote for the young Peggy the song that would weirdly win the Scottish traditionalist a Grammy for song of the year in 1972—and for Roberta Flack, too, for her performance of "The First Time Ever I Saw Your Face." Peggy's version in the 1950s is simple, just banjo and her Appalachian twang. Flack's is Streisand once removed with a bit of soul. It's quite nice, really, a bit overblown. The song itself in its simple version is one of the most time worthy love songs I know. It always reminds me how impossibly hard it is to write a great simple love lyric:

And the first time ever I kissed your mouth
I felt the earth move in my hand
Like the trembling heart of a captive bird
That was there at my command, my love.

MacColl and Seeger recorded dozens of albums, Child albums, protest albums. MacColl was Scottish in background, if not birth, and this showed up. Peggy Seeger wrote some groundbreaking feminist songs, including the great "I'm Gonna Be an Engineer":

Well, I listened to my mother and I joined a typing pool
Listened to my lover and I put him through his school
If I listen to the boss, I'm just a bloody fool
And an underpaid engineer
I been a sucker ever since I was a baby
As a daughter, as a mother, as a lover, as a dear
But I'll fight them as a woman, not a lady
I'll fight them as an engineer!

So, I had my ticket to go see these two. Seeger was still only forty-nine—it's hard to believe she was that young then. And MacColl had turned seventy. He would only live for four more years. But to me they were like folk royalty. I went down to the pub the night of the concert and then upstairs to the room the concert was to be in. I had gotten there pretty early. I'm always arriving early. People say, *Oh, he'll be late to his own funeral.* I suppose they should say of me, *Oh, he'll be early to his own funeral.*

I ran flying after Superman after seeing *It's a Bird . . . It's a Plane . . . It's Superman*, the musical, on Broadway in 1966. Bob Holiday played Superman and Clark Kent. It had a fair amount going for it: music by Charles Strouse, a cast that included Linda Lavin and Jack Cassidy. But it's largely been forgotten. The one hit it produced, which was important at the time, was "You've Got Possibilities." It's an underrated score. In any case, not only was Superman in disguise as Clark Kent, but Clark Kent was in disguise as the actor Bob Holiday, who was trying to go unnoticed as he slipped into a restaurant when I spotted him. The amount of subterfuge I had to see through to catch my autograph mark was equivalent to, say, x-ray vision.

My mother, I believe, voiced some uneasiness about this foray, but I was already off at superspeed, into the restaurant, and legend has it that I asked "Superman" for his autograph. I don't remember this "cute" part. I find it a bit humiliating. I like to think of myself as having been more sophisticated at nine. You know, "Mr. Holiday, fine performance, Old Duff. Keep it up. Don't let the critics get you down. Do us a favor and scribble your John Hancock to this playbill, would you? That's the ticket. Enjoy your meal. You've earned it, sir." He was quite kind, actually, considering the intrusion. We forget sometimes that condescension can have a completely benign connotation—this inflection of the word has largely dropped out of our culture. But yes, Superman treated me with a really charming condescension. That was great. Holiday never really did do much of anything else. He would show up occasionally when the musical was revived. Is everyone who plays Superman, the perfect man, doomed? George Reeves, Christopher Reeve, Bob Holiday . . . Actor's kryptonite.

Some of these stories are confusing to me, both the childhood anecdotes and even the ones of my young manhood, because I think of myself as essentially shy, think that I've always been that way—retiring, even shrinking. At parties I tend to bind to one person like superglue. Mingling means trying desperately not to look awkward. But I realize there is a slight glitch in my self-image when I start telling stories about running after actors into restaurants or when I think about cheekily talking up a transvestite star in a famously raucous nightclub. And I'm not exactly a shrinking violet in my classes, and if I'm reading this essay out loud, now, to an audience, I'm comfortable, I'm enjoying myself in front of the crowd. The personae we create (at least partly) and the personae we think we've created don't always match up. Add to this the emotional nexus, the emotional persona that no one but you may have access to, which reacts to the real or perceived being in the world that marches hither and yon doing things, and you might agree that it's easy to sometimes forget that you aren't so shy or difficult to remember that sometimes you're terribly shy, and sometimes you aren't.

I remember an evening with a poet whose work I love and being told the perfect story. I was having drinks with Robert Creeley in Athens, Ohio. He told me that in the late 1950s he was going to Paris and wanted to meet Samuel Beckett, with whom he shared a publisher. He said he loved Beckett's work. He said he wanted to meet Beckett even though he was a one-eyed American poet that no one had ever heard of. He said he told his publisher that he wanted to meet Beckett even though he was a one-eyed American poet who no one had ever heard of, and his publisher said he would try to set up a meeting. Creeley was to meet Beckett at a bar in Paris. He told me he walked down the stairs, into a grotto of a bar, and Beckett was sitting at table in the back. Creeley joined him, sat down. He said: "Mr. Beckett, I'm just a one-eyed poet who no one has ever heard of, but your work is important to me in the dark corners it takes me to, like this bar. But it's so dark. What keeps you writing?" Beckett told him that he wrote in search of the perfect word, and he said Beckett was *small and round and speckled.*

As a boy, I was small and round and speckled. Now I'm just speckled. My father was booking a group of the New York Jets for a trip somewhere, so my brother and I went with him to meet them at JFK. I must have been about twelve. We had our photo taken with them, my brother holding a football. Just when the photographer was about to take the photograph, one of the Jets pinched my back really hard, the kind of pinch that makes you want to start crying. I don't know if he thought that it would make me laugh or if he was just a sadist. I didn't say anything. I was very good; so many kids are so good at not saying anything.

My narrative antidote was the time we all went to the New York Giants training camp. At the time the Giants had a tight end named Homer Jones— what a wonderful name, American and epic. He was called the fastest man alive. And he was as friendly as could be with us, chatty, tossing us the football and then giving it to us. Afterward, however, we went into the locker room, which was a mistake. I was younger in this story, perhaps seven. The men, among them Fran Tarkenton, were all naked or semi-naked, throwing around their jockstraps. I felt a boyish nausea at all those naked male bodies, all those liberated penises. I wanted them restrained, put back where they belonged, back in the jailhouse of coverage.

When we left, I was torn between two conflicting sentiments (preparation for a life of these): joy at Jones's football and terror at the strange and confusing jones from the locker room.

In a poetry class once with Philip Booth, Philip told a story about Robert Lowell having asked him if the men in submarines were called "submariners." In fact, they are. I was confused by the story because I think it was meant to show a kind of overintellectualized naïveté, but the anecdote didn't really work. We were really impressed, nevertheless, at anything having to do with Robert Lowell. Sometimes it can almost seem like one is having a brush with greatness once removed, as when one's teacher was a friend of Robert Lowell.

I think it feels this way to some of my students when they learn that Ray Carver was my teacher. Ray has become so iconic and has been dead what seems an impossibly long time. I suppose taking classes with Ray was my own brush with greatness, but of course at the time it just felt like taking classes with Ray, who was about as approachable as any significant writer I've known. My favorite Ray story is that when he won a MacArthur award, he immediately went out and bought a new car, a Mercedes. I went over to him at a Joyce Carol Oates reading and asked him what color it was. He said, in his best Ray Carver character voice, "Green, you know, color of money, color of money."

I was also in Ray Carver's class on the night John Gardner died, in 1982. John Gardner had been Ray's teacher and mentor at Chico State. Ray came in looking ashen and told us that Gardner had been in an accident and then dismissed the class. It was a double dose of misery, for the news itself and to know how terrible it must be for Ray.

John Gardner had actually taught at my college, Bennington, several years earlier, and though I hadn't taken a class with him, I talked to him from time to time. Once we were waiting to check books out of the library late at night. John had a large stack. The young woman behind the desk said she couldn't let him take the books without a library card, which he didn't have with him. In a theatrical display of self-mockery, which makes this an anecdote central to my brushery, Gardner said, "Young lady, don't you know who I am?" She looked sheepish. He said, quite loudly, "I'm John Gardner!" I was laughing out loud.

I've met so many writers that I'm all but eliminating them from the narratological maze of this essay. Besides, it's hard to find real greatness in your own field. The stakes are pretty high. Nevertheless, when I was a seventeen-year-old college freshman, my English professor at New York University, a sometimes droll, sometimes silly man (who thought it amusing to say, "The Salad of the Bad Café"), told us one day, when we were reading *Giovanni's Room*, that we were going to have a special guest. And yes, in strolled James Baldwin. Writing this, I still shiver a bit. It's a little like saying, "And then Virginia Woolf spoke to the class for some time" or "We turned to the door, and Fitzgerald sauntered in." If Orwell is sometimes called the "Last Great English Essayist," Baldwin should be considered the "Last Great American Essayist" (apologies to any great living essayists—this requires at least some test of time: you have to be dead). Not to mention the novels. In truth I hardly remember anything he said, I was so stunned at his presence. But I remember that voice—oh, that voice—the most musical American writer's voice, as he leaned against the desk that morning in 1974, when he was fifty, years younger than I am now, and I was waiting for the return of my first college paper, for which I received a C for verbosity.

Right after college I was working as a research assistant for the president of a foundation in New York. I found the whole situation rather odd. I didn't really have any good professional clothes, though I did have a sense of decorum, so I would cobble together some kind of ragtag suit and tie from a cut-rate men's shop, and I had long curly hair like Roger Daltrey and was probably wearing Earth Shoes. I'm sure I looked odd. I worked all that summer of 1978 putting together the statistics for the first Aspen Conference on Lifelong Learning. I suppose I knew how to do that back then. I was paid seventy-five dollars a week. The man I worked for, Alvin Eurich, had been the first chancellor of SUNY and was a former president of Stanford. He was very grandfatherly toward me. When I wasn't at the New York Public Library, just a few blocks away, down Fifth Avenue, I would sit outside his office while all the secretaries walked by and flirted with me, especially a forty-year-old woman named Nellie, who lived up in the Bronx. She kept suggesting I come up and hang out with her and her kids for the weekend. One of the administrators, a Stanford PhD named Carol, would come around and sit on the edge of her desk when I came in to speak with her. She always wore very short skirts. Another woman, named Sydney, a pretty peroxide divorcée, would always wink at me. She must have winked at me twenty or thirty times a day. I had to consciously keep myself from winking back at her. I think I thought that if I did, she would take it as either mockery or the sealing of a pact between us, neither of which I wanted her to infer. All of this made me very nervous and excitable, though none of it amounted to anything.

In the midst of all of this winking and fact gathering, ex-president Gerald Ford came in one day. He just had one person with him, a younger man, aide or agent. That seems right for Ford, to travel so inconspicuously. Eurich came out to greet him and introduced me. "How are you, young man?" "Fine, Mr. President." "Well, you keep up the good work." I assume he meant the good work of being fine. I'm being a bit glib. He was really very nice. There is a strong sense of moment in meeting a former president, even a president who was not particularly prominent. And I had been a complete Watergate hound. Nixon was my personal nemesis for years. This was the man who had pardoned him. But I had forgiven Ford. It was almost impossible not to forgive Ford. He was so obviously decent. I'm glad I got to shake his hand and silently think, "I forgive you, Jerry, for that colossally stupid blunder with Nixon."

When I was sixteen and seventeen, I edited my high school literary magazine with my friend Rob Steele, the man whose name is a tautology. I decided it would be a nice idea to dedicate the magazine (which was full of anti-Nixonia) to Pete Seeger. I sent him a copy, and he sent me a lovely letter back. He urged me to keep up with my writing and suggested that writing could have a real impact on the world. On this last point I really couldn't vouch. He ended the letter with his classic sign-off, "Take it easy, but take it." This was about forty years ago, and Seeger had the mantle of an old man then. He was about my age. I've known one other person who prematurely adopted a geriatric persona—dear Hayden Carruth, whom I also met when he was about my current age but who acted as though he were an old man. Both Seeger, still alive, and Hayden, who died in 2008, had decades to perfect this gerontological persona.

While I'm on a folk music run: I was going to see Arlo Guthrie at Central Park with my high school girlfriend, and she took me over and introduced me to Marjorie Guthrie, Arlo's mother and Woody Guthrie's widow. I was completely thrilled. Wendy had been dancing with Norah, Arlo's sister—that was the immediate connection. But her father had also known Pete Seeger and Woody, had traveled with them years earlier. I was so in the throes of Guthrie and Lead Belly, Cisco Houston, Big Bill Broonzy, Jean Ritchie, Paul Robeson, the Weavers, and the next generation too: the Staples Singers, Joan Baez and early Dylan, Ian and Sylvia, Phil Ochs especially . . . this was a treat that seemed to be more like a gift, a spiritual connection, touching the hand that had touched Woody Guthrie's hand so intimately. Marjorie Guthrie seemed vivacious, warm, solicitous, in the brief moments of our introduction. What is it like to carry the legacy of others, larger than ourselves, to have that aura surrounding you? How much of a burden, I wonder, or does it keep a more benign flame burning, keeping the lost legend close?

Returning to the subject of the less great or not so great, I wonder if I'll show up some day in someone's essay on distance and fame, perhaps one of my student's essays on greatness thrice removed. This professor of mine, David Lazar, was telling a story about Robert Creeley meeting Samuel Beckett. It just so happens that he, David, was small and speckled.

BRIGADOON
BOWLING

I have gradually lost most of my sports over the years, but still, I may be the only person on record to use bowling as a remedy for anxiety. It is my intention to write an essay about bowling. I declare this as a kind of gauntlet and as a way of declaring openly and at the outset my lack of embarrassment as a bowler. When I mention bowling in mixed company, people, especially women, sometimes look at me with a kind of furtive irony, as though I were trying unsuccessfully to speak a private language, slightly unseemly. They think I can't be serious since bowling to some people is a kind of joke sport or not a sport at all but, rather, an "activity," like miniature golf or pinball (which requires its own skill and energies)—things you do when you're really focusing on something else, namely socializing or keeping the kids busy.

But this was not the culture I grew up with in Brooklyn and embraced, surrounding bowling, and I have never lost the sense of the sport, yes sport, as serious enterprise and one for me that became highly self-soothing. But more on that later.

The bowling alleys I grew up with were quiet older alleys, with none of the bells and whistles that are common at today's alleys, which feel something like being inside of a pinball machine. My alley in Brooklyn was Shell Lanes, on homely Bouck Court, near Shell Road, McDonald Avenue, and Avenue

X. The video on their website, which, astonishingly, advertises a snack bar, a game room, a pro shop—all in the same space as the original bowling alley (did they shrink the lanes and turn the balls into marbles?)—says that Shell Lanes is celebrating its fiftieth anniversary, which means I must have started going there when the lanes were pretty new, when I was about ten or so. This surprises me because my memory of Shell Lanes is of a space that seemed a bit well-worn (even with thirty-two lanes, it had the low-ceilinged feel of a union hall or a large Elks room, except, you know, with a lot of noise, as though someone were dropping . . . bowling balls on the floor constantly). Shell Lanes seemed like a relic when I was a kid. There was nothing sixties cool about it. The style was strict midcentury dilapidated.

From the age of ten to sixteen I was captain of my team on the Friday boys' bowling league. Sixteen to seventeen the team name stayed the same, the Knicks (my erstwhile favorite sports team), but it was a mixed-gender league, two boys, two girls. That the league was on Fridays was entirely significant to my adolescence. I loved going bowling so much, despite the occasional bad games or days, that having it to look forward to right after school at the end of the week, during what were frequently weeks of complete misery—those little death threaty episodes that last for years in certain bleak childhood periods—was a saving grace. Yes, I did just aver that: bowling gave my life meaning when I was a boy.

Why? For one thing I had a *team*, and I was the captain! Through much of my adolescence I was fat—I still prefer this to the supposedly politically neutral (though to me it sounds somehow even *worse*) denomination, obese. Even though I played just about every sport and I was reasonably coordinated, my hyper-self-consciousness about how I looked made me fail miserably at most of them, at least until years later, after I had slimmed down. This led to another of the many scourges in my life, constant mockery about my ineptitude and bodily grotesqueness on the playground, which, for some reason, I still did not avoid, it being the place, after all, where I played.

But bowling was reasonably body neutral as sports go. No shorts. No running or jumping. You didn't have to be strong, though some upper body strength didn't hurt. In other words, it was as close as I was apt to get at the time to an even playing field, even though it wasn't a playing field but, rather, an alley made of polished hardwoods.

I don't remember how I became captain—I think it was because I assembled the first ragtag team that signed up for the league, on a kind of whim. It was me and my best friend throughout my adolescence, Rob Steele (first and last name synonyms—I always have to say that, I'm sorry, it's a tic), who remained the two constants on the team throughout the years, with the two other members shifting. At first it was a boy named Billy, who I had a kind of latent crush on for about a year. Between my fatness and his penchant for barely lifting the ball and then winging it into the gutter, we caught a wild and maverick reputation as the "pathetic" team. But since Rob and I were pretty good bowlers—Rob actually very good, I good, and the third bowler sometimes very good too—we were reasonably competitive, since the games were scored with averages and bonus points given to the weaker team. In other words, if we outperformed ourselves, as we frequently did, we had an excellent chance of beating a much better team because we were given those additional points based on the fact that they were so much stronger. It was a way to keep the league competitive, to keep one or two teams from winning over and over and over. But it made the best teams really angry when they lost to a clearly inferior team. We didn't really care, as long as they didn't wait for us outside with the purpose of thrashing us and making us say, on our knees, "I'm just a weakly bowling fool! An over-accommodated rolling impostor!" Well, words to that effect. Avenue X, in Brooklyn, full of bakeries and pizzerias—and Mafiosi—would have spawned more colorful language. But hurting us, which they seemed sometimes to be on the verge of deciding to do after we won, would have bespoken an inability to take the loss that even the most heathenish of our opponents understood. So they left us alone.

Even after I asked Greg to join the team. Greg Uzoaga was a very close friend of mine for a few years. He was black, smart, enigmatic, tough. We would hang out, go to the City together. He was an excellent, if erratic, power bowler. He loved to just slip the ball under the pin return mechanism as it was pulling up, just for fun, sometimes hitting it, even breaking it, which infuriated the managers. But Greg didn't care. He smiled a kind of Mona Lisa smile at everything. He always claimed that his mother was a principal, and this seemed plausible, since I spoke to her a number of times on the phone, and she seemed really smart, and his father was president of Nigeria. This seemed slightly less plausible, simply because. I mean, how did that all work? How did they meet? When did Greg see him? What was Nigeria like? Greg didn't have any answers, by which I mean he wouldn't deign to answer any questions. He would just smile his Mona Lisa smile that said, "Man, you're so stupid—my father is president of Nigeria." I didn't quite believe it, but I bought it, if that makes sense. I bought his routine, I found it attractive, and I liked how tough he was.

But his toughness came with a price at the time. A white kid hanging out with a black kid in my neighborhood was completely verboten. Not that I cared. But Gravesend, especially though not exclusively Italian Gravesend, was completely racist.

So, on the one hand, Greg was tough, a bit bigger than I, and could handle himself. On the other hand, when we walked around, there was this air of implicit violence, and one tough guy plus a puff pastry on two legs wouldn't be much of a match if anything serious developed. One time, especially, it almost did. Greg and I were leaving the bowling alley, and three Mafialettes (children of the mafia, my affectionate nickname for them—yes, sounds like a confection involving eggs and guns) were going through the door at the same time. They were staring us down pretty hard, and as I noted earlier, Greg was rather unyielding in his facial demeanor when pressed. So, they were staring at him as we passed each other, and then he turned around and stopped, and they had stopped, and it was one of those *Man Who Shot Liberty Valance* moments when John Wayne dares Lee Marvin to go for his gun and you think, okay, here comes the action. But after about three very long seconds, we all spontaneously moved on.

"What just happened?" I asked Greg. "Oh, I gave them the backwards flip, and I guess they like it so much," he said drily. "The backwards flip?" It sounded like diving. "Explain," I said. "It's nothing. I just flipped the group of them off behind my back as we were walking past them. I didn't like the way they were looking at me." Greg was like John fucking Wayne to me in that moment. Though I also felt that he might get me killed at some point.

However, he didn't. And Greg passed from my life, just vanished at some point in the way that people disappear when we're young. I don't remember any good-byes or imminent departures. I just remember a period of years when he was in my life, bowling and hanging around, and then the years when he wasn't. There are others like that, too, and those for whom I'm sure I, too, have flickered in that will-o'-the-wisp friendship quality.

So, my bowling time on Fridays, year after year, was a predictable solace of friendship and focused activity that I could excel in. My Knicks team took second place in the league one year, an achievement duly celebrated. And one year Rob and I won, against all odds, the doubles tournament. I bowled three 200-plus games and, in the generous terms of the league, took home nice little trophies for each.

And all the while the lovely dull sound of the acoustics waited for us through those after-school afternoons, which in my memory are always cold, lugging our fetishized bags with balls and shoes through the snow, to that sound of thunder you hear in bowling alleys, ball hitting wood—until it was mostly drowned out, years later, by the electronic clanging of modern alleys. There was something primitive in the sound, dull thud, roll, thud, roll, asynchronous . . . thud, thud, roll, thud, roll, roll . . . and comforting in how basic it seemed. But that basic quality is essential, after all, to the sport and what I prize about it: big heavy ball, ten objects. Throw ball to knock objects down. You figure some version of this started up as soon as we stood up. As Johan Huizinga points out in *Homo Ludens* (Playing Man), games predate culture, as we conventionally define it, and knocking something down with something started really early.

My one time getting in trouble in a class was both caused by and soothed by bowling. I was in Mr. Camiel's math class, algebra, in the seventh grade, and Mr. Camiel was a scary guy, a former Golden Gloves boxer, small but compact and strong. He used to hit kids in the front of the class if they were misbehaving. One time Andy Matroni, a popular kid and captain of the football team but a bit of a fuck-up, a clown in class, walked in at the start of class, and Camiel leaned back and punched him in the arm, really hard. "What was that for, Mr. Camiel?" Camiel, in his dry, slightly Brooklyn Italian accent, said, "Matroni, you'll do something today to justify that." When Matroni committed some absolutely minor offense during class, Camiel stopped and turned to him and said, rather melodramatically, "You see, Matroni?"

I had turned to Rob Steele (first and last names synonyms—really, I'm sorry, it's a bit OCD of me) and said, "Only an hour until bowling," as though a rocket were going to launch or we were about to be sprung from prison, which, thinking back, probably approximates how I felt. The next thing I heard was, "Lazar, get your books, and get out of here." I didn't even try to protest. I think I was afraid to, though, interestingly, Camiel had a knack for hitting only the working-class kids, never the middle-class kids, understanding, no doubt, exactly how far the boundaries of his corporal powers extended. I wandered outside to wait for Rob (note my self-control), since it was last period. Camiel walked past me and said, in utter solicitation and friendliness, "Hey David, make sure you get the homework assignment." It completely confused me at the time. I expected him to be mad at me, like a parent.

I liked bowling so much—its seeming simplicity, surrounded by an individual bowler's tics and style, the fact that great bowlers could be lean and tall, stodgy and short. Some bowlers tap the ball three times before they start their walk down the alley. Some look up (Jesus? Dead mom?). Some all but rush down the lane, while others seem to glide. Some bowlers use a dramatic curve, the ball seeming to hang on the gutter until it swoops toward the pocket. Others roll a more subtle arc. It's actually a game of the most subtle adjustments of the hand, the wrist, the movement of the feet. Jokes about its sociological provenance to the contrary (bowling as a sport of beer and cigarettes, the working-class sport), bowling, I argue, is at its best dancerly. Dancerly, with a twenty-pound piece of plastic that has to be thrown.

I had a very specific style of bowling. But then, everyone did. Bowling may seem somewhat primitive: drop ball, hit objects. But it's actually a game of small adjustments and, for those who take it seriously, infinite fetishes. We could start with the question of the ball itself. It's been years since I've considered these things, but I remember the debate raged at the time between plastic and rubber balls, each having their adherents. Rubber balls were classic, plastic the newer technology. I seem to remember that the idea was you could get better speed and more of a certain kind of spin with plastic, but as with many things, such as the trajectory of my life, I may be inventing that out of material from other sources. I had two or three beloved bowling balls (and yes, let's just acknowledge and dispense with the scrotal jokes that even we adolescent Brooklyn boys tired of by fifteen): one fairly light and multicolored that I think some of the other bowlers saw as a kind of stupid confection but with which I could strike a lot when I happened to be accurate; and then the ball I had from about fifteen or sixteen until, well, now. A subtle silver planet, a sci-fi haze of a ball, it was quite heavy, for me at least—about sixteen pounds—and I could bowl very consistently with it. I started averaging about 150 to 160, which isn't bad.

I threw the ball without a curve, which is unusual for bowlers, and with backspin, which is all but unheard of, since it's virtually impossible to hit the pocket, the space between the head pin (1 pin) and the 3 pin if you're right-handed, where you're most likely to get a strike. The way I bowled, my ball would frequently start left and then start spinning back right, so if it hit the "pocket," it was likely to hit it on the left side (the 1 and 2 pins), ideal for a left-handed strike. When a right-handed bowler gets a strike this way, it's called a "Brooklyn," probably because it's kind of a nutty way to make a strike, in keeping with the historical character of the home borough.

I don't know why I bowled that way. And I tried to change it, but that always made things worse, terrible. I ended up looking disabled.

The number of steps a bowler takes, his approach, is also very important. Some bowlers only take three or four steps. Some, such as I, begin right at the foot of the alley. I took a lot of little complicated steps. I'm not sure if I was trying to be the Fred Astaire of the bowling crowd—a rather dubious desire, I would think, in the crowd I ran with—but I was pretty twinkly and fleet and complicated in getting that sixteen-pound piece of plastic flung down the hardwoods. So much so that occasionally something in my developing adolescent brain misfired and I forgot how to dance down the alley. In other words, my steps were so complicated that I sometimes, especially if I were having a somber adolescent day, forgot them. Again, I don't know how or when or why I developed my Balanchine approach. Some guys just took two or three basic steps and flung their balls. Their games certainly didn't suffer from it. Perhaps I was doing what became a kind of life motif, the opposite of a carpe diem. (What is the opposite of a carpe diem? Well, it could be a *carpe diem cras*, seize the day tomorrow, which could be the motto of procrastinators. Another possibility might be *amitte diem* or *amitte occasionem*, let the day slip by or let the opportunity slip by). In any case it was a perpetual delay of what I was unsure of, though with some flair, some style. Is that it? Was I the jaunty procrastinator, hiding his anxiety behind a bit of artful cadenced stepping and sliding? This begins to sound like writing, of course, and brings me head on to where I began.

Bowling and writing are connected to me most viscerally, and if bowling was the release for my anxiety throughout my childhood, and continued to be for years afterward, it also was the occasion for a crisis in which I first took writing seriously. I was fourteen or so, the age when I forced my body into the cataclysmic metamorphosis (I first wrote metaphor!) in which I shed a third of my weight. On one spring night during this transformation, we were in a very close game with a team that was particularly nasty—taunting, close to threatening. For kids who weren't cool, we were usually surprisingly cool in those circumstances. Simply because we knew weren't going to get pummeled in a bowling alley. Any other kind of alley, and we would have been offering the keys to our parental homes. Just for starters.

But on this night the combination of my own angst and the invective threw me off, and I . . . just couldn't make my way down the alley. It was as though a string kept pulling me back or an eraser would wipe away the memory of my steps each time I tried to put one foot in front of the other. To finish the frame, I just walked forward and stood at the foul line and threw the ball down the alley, wildly. I went and got my coat and ball and went home, silencing everyone, who couldn't believe I was just walking out and, by doing so, forfeiting the match.

I felt humiliated and completely confused. I didn't understand why my body had betrayed me. In the happiness of my dark fourteen-year-old room, my dark fourteen-year-old soul, I did what perhaps some of you did under other circumstances. Which is to say circumstances that didn't involve a bowling alley. I started writing poems. I wrote several that night. And I never stopped. They were predictably terrible, and unfortunately, none of them were about bowling. That might have been marvelous, novel! But it's what got me started. The next week I could bowl again.

Over the years when a pitch of anxiety would grab me, yes, sometimes I write, though writing is usually not my response to anything other than my imperative to write. Sometimes tautologies succeed where ideologies falter.

Frequently over the years, I would, especially in the afternoons, when the demons seemed to be more full of hauteur than usual, find my way to a favorite bowling alley and bowl three games. Bowling in the afternoon is really quite delightful. It's the ultimately hooky. Very few adults think to go bowling in the afternoons during the week (perhaps because they're working or some such thing), and so the lanes are pretty quiet. I like bowling by myself. Bowling with other people is slightly awkward if they're bowlers who think bowling is this goofy activity that's mostly about beer and screaming if you happen to get a strike. If you actually like *bowling itself*—the small adjustments of release, the sound of a perfect strike, or the wild geometry of a difficult spare—bowling alone is frequently the best option.

Why would I bowl—why that as opposed to, say, a walk in the park, a matinee, a pinch of nectar? I enjoy all of those things, too, but bowling, I think, has been able to reconnect me to a rhythmically balanced self of myself in a way that nothing else could. Ironically, the thing that could so throw me out of balance later became the thing that could restore it. I breathe, holding that heavy ball, I start to stride, and then release. I focus on what I have to do, what my body has to do. I don't claim to fully understand it. Call it my Zen of bowling. But it has always worked rather nicely to make me feel that God's in his heaven (so to speak) and the pins are in the underworld, where I have sent them.

But as I noted earlier, it's gotten harder and harder to find a wonderful alley, since all the new ones are geared to pinball bowlers. I don't think I'll ever find—or, wait, let's shoot for a bit of optimism—I only hope to one day find a bowling alley like the one I used to visit in Lancaster, Ohio, on my drives between Ohio University, where I was teaching, and Canal Winchester, just outside of Columbus, where I was living. I had blundered across these lanes one time while looking for a possible school for my son. It was tucked away in the hills overlooking Lancaster and just about impossible to find unless you knew about it. Lancaster Lanes had sixteen lanes all in a row, lovely original walnut paneling from the late 1940s or early 1950s and a tiki bar that was always open in the afternoon. They very softly played old standards: Rosemary Clooney, Dean Martin, Frank Sinatra, Peggy Lee. And in the afternoons, when I stopped in on my way home from teaching, there were always only two or three couples in their late middle age or older, quietly rolling games. No electronics. It was like a balm to whatever was on my mind. I could never lose my steps in Lancaster Lanes. One day I was there, bowling my middle game and bowling rather superlatively. I had bowled a 200-something my first game and was on way to another, which I had never done. I was sipping on a gin and tonic in my little red plastic cup. I looked outside the big bay window near the front. I was on one of the rear lanes, and I could see a heavy Ohio snow coming down, and I felt as though I were in a little bowling snow globe—like it was Brigadoon Bowling I had stumbled across and if I left this perfect place, I'd never find my way back. Anxiety? What was that?

These days I find my relief less often. I live in Chicago, and the big lanes are just too . . . big and loud for me. Friends tell me of little hideaways, semi-mythological lanes stuck in the back of bars. These sound rather too cloistered for my tastes. If anyone knows of a pretty little alley close to the city, I'd be indebted for a call. Don't email me. This should be recherché. Just give me a call, speak the name of the alley, and hang up. Know that I'll hold you dear to my heart and that my heart, too, will be the better for it. I'll go there alone, go through my paces, knowing I still know the steps.

FIVE AUTOBIOGRAPHICAL
FRAGMENTS, OR SHE MAY
HAVE BEEN A WITCH

1. SHE MAY HAVE BEEN A WITCH

I was playing outside my house in Brooklyn on a summer day, under the big oak tree that seemed to symbolize time: it must have been there forever, and it *must* be there forever; it was so old and impossibly rooted, so fixed. A very old woman walked past me and looked at me with what I thought was evil power, the power to hold me or hurt me. She was dressed in tatters, hunched, stock figured for nursery rhyme caricature for a little boy or some little boys. To other little boys she was probably the woman next door or Aunt Agnes. Of course, she may have been a witch. I thought she was a witch but didn't want to think she was a witch. She walked down the street, and I felt transfixed by her power. She didn't turn around. But I said to myself, if she turns around when she gets to the corner and looks at me, she's a witch. She knows what I'm thinking. I had projected such extraordinary power onto her, because she seemed so different from the world of my day, or the day of my world, or perhaps because I was terribly upset about something, a broken toy, a misdemeanor, a wayward thought that couldn't be corralled or corrected, and so I projected the trouble, the problem, the powerful feelings, onto this hunched, beleaguered-looking figure who, after all, probably had cast a sidelong glance at me and thought painfully how rotten age was, how little respite from pain and responsibility, as she trudged down the street, and still after all these years never any money. Of course, she may have been a witch.

I stood in the middle of a square of concrete, and it felt as though I couldn't breathe. She was halfway, now two-thirds of the way down to the end of the next block, where she must cross the avenue, Avenue Z, the alphabetical land's end, where she would cross the divide to, well, another series of marked streets, headed toward the ocean a few blocks down. Would she stop and turn and prove herself a witch? And if she did, what would that mean for me, what was I to do? She came to the curb and stopped, since the light was against her, as I felt everything was against me. I felt, in my body, a heaviness, as though I had lost control, as though I were a witness seeing out of a vessel I were occupying, rather than being that vessel, which I had been only moments earlier. And then, very slowly, as though foreordained, and moving with a desperately smooth and slow fluidity, she turned around. She stared at me from a block away. And then she turned back and walked on.

I was doomed then. What I feared was what I foresaw, and that's just what happened. Even as a child, I realized it made no sense to tell an adult I had seen a witch and was drawn into her power. Though I did anyway. I was not much consoled. My instincts were correct for the second time in a day, once based on the irrational and evil forces of the world and once based on logic and experience. I shivered my way through the coming months and have thought of her now for many decades, this old witch who not even the benign spirit of my timeless tree could protect me from. I still wait for her to do me harm.

2. INSOMNIA 101

Some sadist told me this story when I was about ten or eleven:

There was a boy, and one night he dreamed he was going to be stabbed, but he woke up. The next night he had the dream again, except that the knife drew closer. Well, he had the dream over and over again, and each time the knife would get just a little closer. The boy would wake up in a sweat but relieved that he was released from the terrifying dream. He spoke to his parents, who took him to see their family doctor. The doctor tried to reassure him: "It's only a dream. It can't hurt you. Think pleasant thoughts, and the dream will go away. And no matter what, don't worry. It's only a dream." But the dreams continued, each night the knife getting closer and closer. Finally, the knife was just a hair away. The boy was really quite hysterical. He did everything he could to avoid going to sleep, but eventually the demands of the body overtook him, and he grew weary and fell asleep. The next morning he didn't wake up at the usual time for school. His mother went into his bedroom and checked on him and to her horror found him cold, dead in his bed, a terrible grimace on his face. They performed an autopsy and determined that the boy had died of a heart attack. Stricken, the boy's parents talked to his doctor about what could have caused their otherwise healthy son to take a fatal turn. The doctor paused and said, "Well, you remember those dreams and how I told your son not to worry about them? Well, what I think was that the night he died, the knife finally reached him. The point had just about made it to his abdomen the last time we spoke. Well, on his last night I think the knife went in. He couldn't bear it. The dream killed him."

I don't remember exactly who told me this, but my guess would be an uncle, and I can more or less narrow it down to the ranks of ever insensitive relatives on my father's side, who confused truth and discretion, stories and verities, consolations and clichés, and in fact had very little mechanism for determining what might be the appropriate, interesting, or even passably acceptable thing to say on any given occasion, so of course they thought telling a preadolescent a Poe-like tale in the guise of True Life Horror Stories about how going to sleep will kill you sounded like a capital idea. Well, class, can we guess what happened? Shall we glance again at my title? I couldn't sleep. I wouldn't sleep.

At first I was merely terrified. And then, when a calmer mien descended, I found that the psyche had lowered a kind of cloak of protection upon my body. My psychic horror, not defeatable by its rational gambits, was short-circuited by sleeplessness. But there was a residual effect. I couldn't sleep even when I really wanted to, even when I thought I wasn't scared anymore. At times I worried about whether I would ever sleep again. My family lived in such close quarters that life was uncomfortable in the wee small hours. I grew bored with lying in bed and rehearsing my eleven-year-old thoughts. I hadn't reached the age of self-fascination.

I would sometimes tiptoe into the living room, steps away from our bedroom, and try reading for a while or putting the TV on so low that it was almost like watching silent films. I've always remembered that the movies series they ran at the time, which I may never have known otherwise, was called *The Milk Man's Matinee*, since 4:00 a.m. was about the time the milkmen were doing their rounds. It had a sweet big bandish theme song to go with it.

Sometimes my father would catch me and get very mad. My father never needed much of an excuse for getting mad. He would yell that I was disturbing the "whole house"—I always liked that phrase, *the whole house*, as though the structure itself were being put out by my quietly watching the television in the dark. But by his yelling, ironically, he would wake the whole house. The homes we grow up in are factories of illogic. It would then behoove me to scurry back to bed to preserve my waking life.

When I visit my father, who is pushing ninety-seven and has been hard of hearing for years, he blares the drive-in-movie-sized television in the living room so loud it sounds like the engines of a turboprop. Once, when my son was very small and I was trying to get him to sleep, I suggested that my father turn down the volume. "But how am I supposed to hear the TV?" he said. So much for the whole house.

Nevertheless, watching films—with the volume soft or medium, those flickering pictures in the middle of the night—as a way of soothing my early insomniacal tendencies became a habit, became talismanic. When I was released to my own room on another floor of the house, a bequeathal of grandparental death when I was almost thirteen, a little nine-inch Sony TV accompanied me. I pressed my face against it in bed—the screen was so small—and went to sleep every night with my eyes just inches away from Fred and Ginger, Bette and Ida, Charles and Ronald, John Garfield.

Ironically enough, it's still a Sony but no longer very small, and it's still the way I go to sleep almost half a century later, to calm my anxieties, not of a knife coming at me as I sleep but of the sharp edges of the waking world, the world outside of the movies, the movies . . . where I have lived such a charmed, if double, life.

3. VERY DEEP SNOW

I was walking in very very deep snow. I was in fourth grade, so that means I was eight or nine years old, and it was the winter of 1966. I'm sure the amount of snow isn't amplified memory because there was a terrific blizzard that hit the Northeast the end of that January, a historic nor'easter. The snow fell on and off for days apparently, beginning the day before my birthday, on January 27—though I have no memory of this—and continuing for several days. It's considered the worst blizzard not to hit the City but Upstate New York, with over a hundred inches of snow falling on Oswego in those four days. Syracuse got ninety-six inches. And winds, astonishingly, tried to make the entire region beg for submission with gusts ranging from sixty to a hundred miles an hour. Two of the Finger Lakes got frostbite.

But I was in Brooklyn, in a neighborhood quaintly called Gravesend, walking in very deep snow. Gravesend, for those of you with a passing knowledge of Brooklyn, is at the far end of Brooklyn, not very far from neighborhoods you might know: Flatbush roughly to the north, Coney Island to the south. It's less than five square miles, from Avenue P to Avenue Z and from, according to which map you use, Ocean Parkway, the street I grew up on, a tree-lined thoroughfare designed by Frederick Law Olmsted, to Bay Parkway. Gravesend, which may derive from the Dutch *Grafes Ande*, meaning "end of the grove" or "count's beach," may on the other hand be named after its English namesake. It was the first piece of land chartered by a woman in the New World, Lady Deborah Moody, who couldn't take the Massachusetts Bay Colony and so led a group to, yes, Brooklyn, in 1645. She's responsible for having planned my neighborhood, a fact that has given me a surfeit of pleasure for many years. In these less than five square miles are approximately 150,000 people.

And in 1966, on a very snowy day, I was walking home from school. I had an old crank of a teacher, Mrs. Edison, the old schoolmarm variety, who contrasted completely with my young, warm, and energetic third-grade teacher, Mrs. Gemake. I wonder why it gives us so much pleasure to remember the names of primary school teachers. Do we think we aren't supposed to, that memory should strain to come up with a name for these (back then and even mostly now) women whose care we were in for nine months of a given year? I remember nothing from fourth grade except for three things: Mrs. Edison fiercely (and rather ineffectually) yelling at the class; putting Elmer's Glue on my hand and experiencing a deep, almost sexual pleasure at peeling it off (I did this over and over again, well, masturbatorily); and building, along with my male *confères*, strange and complicated airships made of rulers and pencils, rubber bands and erasers. We did this last activity out of view, under our desks, and consequently never listened to Mrs. Edison, who consequently was always yelling at us. I think what we had there was a vicious circle.

In 1966, on a very snowy day, I had built an especially good airship. It had outdone anything I had imagined I could do. I loved it with a fierce pride. I suppose this is the fifth element of memory from that year. I couldn't wait to walk home through the snow to show it to my mother, since showing things to my mother, displaying my genius for these things and having her radiance shine on me, was pretty much what I lived for, especially since I generally experienced myself as a mediocre wretch.

I went trudging through the snow, the very deep snow. It's curious how vividly, how presently, I can remember this next part of the memory. I am holding my prize in one hand, walking down Manhattan Court, the last block before the turn onto Ocean Parkway and steps to my house. I have my books in my other hand, tied together with a rubber strap, which we used to use back then in lieu of a bag. Strangely, there is absolutely no one around—I am the only little snow person on the street, or in the world, as though the snow was just a foretaste of something else to come that made everyone huddle inside for fear. And then my right hand is holding nothing, is holding air.

How can this be? I am bringing home my prize, the great contraption; I am on my way to collect my share of radiance. My hand just held the grail;

how can it be empty? I stopped. I looked behind me. I looked in front of me. I felt, in my unarticulated ten-year-old way, that I had experienced the impossible or had stepped through to some other world, some other place or time. It was just in my hand, and it must be there, but it is not there. I turned and retraced my steps in an uncontained panic. Nothing. I was already feeling that it was the object that I loved more than any other object I had ever briefly had.

So, it was cognitive dissonance in the cold and snow, along with, quite immediately, that pang of loss—in this case strange loss. I had to stop looking at some point. It was nearly February, so nearly dark in the late afternoon. I trudged on home in desperate need of my mother's other magic power, consolation, though I knew it would be insufficient this time, and it was; when I reached the door and uttered my lament, a great oxymoron of surfeiting warmth and cold comfort came from her to me, for I had lost my prize, or some snow devil had grabbed it, grabbed it while I wasn't looking, and disappeared in the remnants of that very snowy day.

4. STATION

It's still hard for me to come to grips with the number of times I was robbed, mugged, and hassled as a child growing up in New York. At some point I even became rather nonchalant about it. As a father of an adolescent boy, I find it startling to think of the things I did when I was thirteen or fourteen in Brooklyn and Manhattan—the places I used to go by myself or with a friend, my mother having no idea where I was for the day, riding the trains by myself. That made for a very citified boy, and I've always liked that side of me, the side that's comfortable in almost any urban environment, because I ventured out so young. But the downside, the price, was: robbery with knives pulled, being punched in the face because I wouldn't give a stranger a dollar, having my coat pulled at for a block by a desperate rummy who was trying to shake me down, and some aggressive homosexual come-ons that I wasn't schooled for. Robbery seemed more familiar. After all, even our house was robbed twice. But as John Dewey says, you learn through experience, and I certainly had some.

When I was thirteen, I was in Penn Station, which was across from my father's office. Penn Station, architectural abomination that it is, resides under Madison Square Garden, and it's like an enormous bomb shelter with terrible restaurants, kitschy shops, and, in its bowels, rail lines. It used to be one of the great grand stations of the country, equal to Grand Central. But instead of being declared an architectural monument, it foolishly was torn down in 1963 (a fate that Grand Central almost met, if you can imagine), and in its place they built the new Garden and the new station, which really only makes aesthetic sense as a gateway to New Jersey. The bathrooms nearest the trains were right off Seventh Avenue, and at a young age I already knew they were the court of last resort, the place to "go" only if tide and time had conspired against you with finality, since dilapidation bred danger. That did sometimes happen. The bathrooms were full of homeless men and shady characters—I'm sure guys were shooting up in there—men washing, a constant river on the floor, and the ever-present stench of the exquisite gestalt of the body's deterioration mixed with its demise.

I had to go. So I went. I stood before a urinal. And midway through my session of relief, a man threw himself on the floor next to me in a gesture of fellatio. He grabbed at me, and I spun around, doing who knows what damage to my clothes, and ran like crazy out of the bathroom. I'm sure I must have shouted something unintelligible, like "Hey! What!" It upset and confused me, though it isn't like I didn't *understand* it. I became utterly gay friendly very early, in the flowering of my political self, when I was fifteen, sixteen, seventeen, but I'd be lying to say, at that tender age, that I wasn't disgusted. I worried that even thinking about the experience would tarnish me. I calmed down, though, and realized that in the worst of times some bathrooms are best left unexplored.

About a year later I was going to go into Manhattan, on one of my regular jaunts, to visit the arcades and go to a game show on a Saturday morning. I was taking the N train at the Sea Beach station, not my usual stop, on a cloudy, indifferent kind of fall day. No one around. I was going to meet my friend Greg Uzoaga at the next stop. I was the only person on the platform—most of the traffic to the city on the trains was commuters and young couples and kids going into the city on weekend nights. Other times it was really pretty slow.

As I waited, a man came shuffling along up the stairs, and he looked like stock casting of the kind of guy I didn't want to get within ten feet of. He had a rumpled raincoat, heavy black shoes, a version of a fedora that had seen better days, with stains so visible you could try to guess if they looked more like Texas, California, or Wyoming. I paid him no mind, but he came and stood about five feet from me—much too close on a deserted platform—and, after a very brief few moments, began conversing.

I was then, and am still, not the friendliest person around and about the city—well, or really anywhere. I'm not particularly *unfriendly*, just not friendly. As a city child, you became so inured to the ways people can interrupt your progress through the urban world that you just adopt a posture of virtual deafness and almost immutable solitariness as you move through the city. It's the role of the flaneur—watch but don't get close; preserve your anonymity. This has never left me. I will never strike up a conversation with the person sitting next to me on the train, at the table next to me, in the seat next to me on an airplane. I'm sure that friendliness is a groovy strategy for many people, but my own isolation is comfortable and inviolable. Unless, of course, under the most rigorous and specific circumstances, someone initiates contact with me with enough of a come-hither to make me leave my well-carved shell.

This gentleman spoke to me. He said it was kind of a nasty day, which I remember thinking was an overstatement, since it was merely cloudy, though in retrospect I like to think that he was subconsciously passing judgment on himself. I said something like "I guess"—something nonresponsive. "Where you going?" "The City." There were a few of these back-and-forths. I didn't like him. I didn't like being chatted up. I didn't like being stood next to with less than twenty feet of distance by a man in a raincoat on a deserted platform. Then he went in for the kill, and I could smell it a mile away. "You got a girlfriend?" I should have just said yes, but some preternatural instinct toward honesty, unavailable in other situations where I had proven myself a capable enough liar, asserted itself, perhaps because in sensing his low road, I was willing myself high.

"Do you like boys?"

"I have friends. I have friends that I like." I believe I stuttered a bit on this one.

"I like boys. I like it when they suck me off."

I experienced this rather viscerally—it was more than I had expected. My heart was racing. But in the moment, especially in cities, we perform a calculus based on experience and instinct, one of which is survival. I willed myself to remain unruffled, to show not a shred of alarm or concern. But in a completely calm and balanced voice, I said, "Go to the end of the platform, or I'm going to push you in front of the train." He looked at me, shall we say, askance. So, I said, more forcefully and unconditionally, "I'm going to push you in front of the train." He turned and started walking toward the end of the platform. And soon after the train came.

Then, and now, my sense of innocence is outraged by the older man preying on the boy, though (rain down your horror on me, hypocrite reader!) I feel the urge to historicize some of the purity of my censure with an eye on how culturally relative are the taboos and mores regarding commerce between the ages. As much of a wretch as the stock figure in the raincoat may have been, it was around the same time, the same age, that I began stealing money from my mother to visit both the charming and sordid brothels of Manhattan. Is it less horrifying to think of the boy in thrall to the older woman in a room than crouched in the corner of a train station with an older man? Does it matter who initiates the encounter, their sexual orientation? Yes, I was straight, but is that not largely an aesthetic distinction in this context? Had the solicitation been from a woman in a raincoat, even reasonably attractive, I believe I would have missed my train. And that, as the poet says, would have made no difference at all, except perhaps for this story and maybe Greg Uzoaga.

5. FIVE

I am playing with the petals of a white flower, which is obtruding from the fence of my neighbor's yard, on a warm summer morning. I am very young, perhaps five years old. Why have I returned to this moment so often over the years? In his essay on screen memory, Freud writes of the enigma at the heart of seemingly unimportant moments that lodge in our memories, those "mnemic images whose innocence makes them so mysterious." He comments, "I feel surprised at forgetting something important, and I feel even more surprised, perhaps, at remembering something apparently indifferent." But Freud writes that out of "apparent innocence" the memory hides an early injury to the ego, probably some event contiguous to the memory that has been effaced and replaced by the memory that has been retained. The replacement memory itself is not pure but is constructed at a later, more sexualized time out of earlier "traces." The screen memory serves a double function then: repressing either trauma or desire and replaying the repressed (the classic return of the repressed) memory in the reprocessed form of the more soothing screen.

Should we accept Freud's version of memory—and I've always found it compelling—our only access past the sureties of the screen's complacency is through language. The warmth of the morning, the protrusion of the white flower through the fence, and its fingering. It's a very sexualized image, true. But really, I can go not much further than that.

Screen memories work as a kind of double discourse. Freud writes, "Two psychical forces are concerned in bringing about memories of this sort. One of these forces takes the importance of the experience as a motive for seeking to remember it, while the other—a resistance—tries to prevent any such preference from being shown." It is this tension that fascinates me, and it was so culturally radical. Where would we be, where would I be, were it not for the wavering memory, the self-doubt, the deconstruction of self that accompanies each foray into the past?

But then, another thought occurs to me. Has this memory stayed with me, did it first stir me, as the trickster spur of thinking about memory itself? Has that, too, not been a constant screen, my Scheherazade of possible motives? Or is it Salome? Sometimes I feel like I'm dancing around my own head. In any case, if so, what a charming masquerade; what a pleasant feint to help one's life work along. And how warm the sun, how white the white flower, that morning half a century ago.

PANDORA AND THE
NAKED DEAD WOMAN

I have boxes I haven't opened in years, and they're starting to feel like Pandora's. On a dating website one of the questions I was asked and chose to answer was, "Would someone going through your things after your death be surprised or shocked at what they found?" My first response, "Who is going to bother?" wasn't an option, so the next closest to what I think of as true would be yes. Partially because I no longer have a clear idea of what's in the boxes and partially because I do. There are boxes of correspondence—you know, those things we used to send each other written with pen or pencil, flown on airplanes, hand delivered. Some of these date from my teens, or the 1970s, for those of you who don't know my REAL age. I actually lie my age up a little bit usually so people will take pity on me, which feels exhilaratingly strange since a couple of years ago I was an angry young man. Well, not that angry. But very very anxious. In any case I will sometimes mutter my age plus five in mixed company to try to get served the first cocktail, that sort of thing, but I think I don't generally overdo it.

I think this is the first time I've marked myself as "older" in an essay, and it makes me a little queasy. As in I don't want to be. That. But I've just turned fifty-nine, so I need to play with my age as a way of loosening the grip of my sense of terror. All right, I think I've done that. Back to the letters.

I used to write them promiscuously, as I'm sure many of you did who matured before email. I even had a pen pal for decades. Decades! A slip of paper given to me in French class in eighth grade and letters and visits were exchanged, in London, New York, Paris, Saintes . . . but that should be an essay in itself. As might be the box of letters I have from my high school girlfriend, my first love. In our summer of love, not 1967 but 1974, her parents were so intent on creating some time and space between us that they took her to South America for a month. We were horrified at the idea of being apart for thirty days, in the way that only teenagers in love can be. To salve our panic, we each wrote thirty letters to each other, one for every day we were going to be apart, a letter a day to be opened . . . I still have that box of letters in a box of letters, can remember its color, the torn cardboard edges . . . It's almost too dear for me to muse too long over now without feeling a kind of weight of distant sweetness, a burdened oxymoron of the past.

But I wrote letters to almost everyone I knew from my teens to the letter-killing email arrival in the 1990s—friends, lovers, parents, teachers—and they wrote back, and I've kept almost all the letters I received. What's most disquieting, what would be and what was, the last time I peeked into a box of correspondence, are letters, passionate letters, from women I no longer remember. Some refer to weekends, promising days ahead . . . and I'm just blank. Well, not completely, the names bring images up from a projector that's been dropped from a third-story window. You blink and shake your head trying to catch the image, sure the image must be capturable, but give up, realizing the equipment is too damaged; you'll never see her again, unless you played with memory's anachronism fire—went to the Internet, to Facebook or something, and looked her up. What's the fun in restoring a lost memory when you can rest in the consideration of the damage, the loss? We've lost all kinds of loss in our ability to find things with such immediacy. I want to encourage, to embrace myself, a new reluctance toward our emotional prosthetics—memory for me being never neutral—and suggest we let some things go. Let's call it a society of the Luddites of Loss.

I'm sure if I read through these letters, there would be no end to surprises, all kinds of things about my youngers selves I'd learn. I'm surprised that anyone could not be surprised by their younger selves! Is the society of changelings so select? Do people imagine themselves as so consistent in their narrative progression? No wonder everyone's reading memoirs. I wouldn't be surprised at all to read a letter from my twenty-year-old self and find depths of sincerity and wit that would make me seem churlish now! Who was that remarkable lad? I might say, since I'm apt to talk that way when I'm writing the kind of things I imagine myself saying. And what terrible things befell him that he became me! He seemed so sweetly inchoate, so wise-embryonic, that surely something I've forgotten must have thrown him off-track. A virus perchance? A miasma?

But the letters are not the only thing in those boxes, the boxes under the stairs and in the furnace room, sitting precariously on the shelves in the laundry room. I don't have a basement, so I have boxes everywhere one can think to put a box. Sometimes I shed a tear, and a tiny little box falls out of my eye with paper clips and ephemera spilling out of the top. I never manage to get it back in. I have two boxes of books sitting in my office from my last move seven years ago. I don't have the bookshelf room for them. They sit there forlornly, daring me, every day, to open them and see what I've imprisoned in the dark all these years. Aldous Huxley perhaps? I have noticed him gallivanting on the shelves. Or maybe Dorothy Richardson, her books slipping from a long nap to a deep coma.

To return to my opening gambit, there is more than books and letters in the boxes. I have lots of these marvelous things called photographs. Photographs used to be printed pieces of paper with captured images of people or things, made with a machine called a camera, which really means a room, a chamber. Frequently these images were of people we knew, even people we liked. Taking photographs of people we despised was always a tricky business. For one thing they rarely responded when we said, "Smile, you little minx." But these people we liked, even loved—relatives, friends, lovers—would indulge us while we eternalized their image or at least captured it for as long as the material photograph lasted. This wasn't perhaps much longer than the life of the photographer, frequently, since the value of the photograph wasn't usually seen as aesthetic but personal, even though, as a genre, the personal photograph certainly has its devices, its charms, its own accidental moments of genius. See Roland Barthes. See Marianne Hirsch. They'll tell you lots of interesting things about the casual, the amateur, the family photograph.

I had boxes of these, yes, and these tended to be a little less lonely than many of the others, batches of photos occasionally grabbed to be viewed when I was in a chaotically sentimental mood. When I wanted to see glimpses of the past through the lens, as it were, of the images that had been produced by my lens. This was frequently a disconcerting experience, since I have never arranged my photographs. I am predisposed to have my memorabilia echo my memory: fragmented, out of sequence, disjointed, lacking revelation. So, I would grab handfuls of photos from a box and riff through them: a photograph of me at age five in the Catskill Mountains would be followed by my mother in a gold lamé evening dress descending the metal stairs of a row house garden scene; this in turn would have as a chaser the image of my friend, hair poofing out the sides of his head like a black Irish Afro, in Colorado, perhaps thirty-five years ago, looking all intense and young poety, as though he were accusing me of not taking his photo interestingly enough.

And so a kind of narrative emerges, though making sense of it is a bit like reading Krazy Kat or watching early Max Fleischer cartoons.

And the next photograph, and the three after that, you find to your dismay, are pictures of a dead naked woman.

A woman who was then about thirty-five years old. I'll tell you with some discretion what's in the photographs and what I remember of the setting. They take place in my house in Ohio, when I was a young professor there. These are late-night Polaroids—Polaroids! How *recherché*! And this was clearly a night of some debauchery. *Debauchery* is a wonderful word. It derives from the Middle French *debaucher*, "to entice from work," and the Old French *desbaucher*, "to lead astray," both of which suggest a pale sense of the dark carnival the word has always represented to me. Ironically, it is the older, more obscure etymological elements that come closer to the essence, I think. *Bauch*, or "beam," is Frankish, if not all that frank, and has the literal meaning of making a beam by trimming wood, by stripping it away. It is that stripping away, and the trim, that leads me to the brink of the word's sharp connotations, the exquisite sense of searching for some core version of your nastiest self. And yes, on that night the woman in the photograph and I had stripped down considerably, literally and metaphorically, as we filled up capriciously and injudiciously, probably with gin, on our way to, if memory serves me, a night of sex, accusations, and naked Polaroids. We debauched, which is my way of saying we had less fun than we actually wanted, and probably did more than we planned.

If memory serves me. Does memory serve me? How does memory serve me? When does memory serve me? When does memory fail me? Well, frequently, but I mean emotionally. But to return to the first question: if memory serves. Literally, we mean *if I remember correctly*. A kind of poeticized hedge against memory's inevitable faultiness. *If.* If as usual memory is leading me down a garden path . . . If memory is toying with me for the sake of some subconscious masochistic motive that I'm not aware of . . . If memory is anything at all other than something I started making up yesterday and I'm almost finished fabricating . . . *If memory serves*. Does memory serve? In Miltonic terms I tend to think memory is *non serviam*. Which is to say, I suppose, I have a devilish time remembering whether memory's floors have been cleaned lately of all the dust and rubbish that have blown in and lain about while the house was not so slowly sliding into disrepair.

She sits in a high backed wicker chair, wearing sheer black underwear, just bottoms, her eyes a bit glazed, though not unhappy, staring vaguely at the bay window. The woman in question, a former love, is dead, dead by her own hand two years ago now. I suppose if I had found the photos ten years ago, even the demi-glace of the night in her eyes—mine of course only recorded in the ever-so-slight shake of the camera (or was that just desire) when the picture was recorded—would still have been found when Pandora threw these photos up for my dark delectation some space for erotic contemplation (but did Pandora reveal the photographs, or are the photographs of Pandora herself?). That's a complicated way of saying that even with the passage of time, I would have been aroused, memory serving me a slice of juicy peach pie, of debauchery warmed over. But it's difficult for me to feel the frisson of past arousal, of past frenetic escapading, with a dead woman.

Not because it is impossible, in truth. But because it is accompanied by a storm of sorrow that estranges it into strangeness. Necrophiliacal memory, you don't serve me. Though others, I imagine, might not be tamed, so awed in erotic submission by something as petty as death, as suicide—alas, I am weak and too subject to the whims of my mortal imagination.

Thomas Browne is the first writer on record to use the word *suicide*, in *Religio Medici*, 1643. I never tire of Browne, his strange, morbid asides and meditations, peculiar, baroque, melancholy. He writes, in the "Fragment on Mummies":

> Death, that fatal necessity which so many would overlook, or blinkingly survey, the old Egyptians held continually before their eyes. Their embalmed ancestors they carried about at their banquets, holding them still a part of their families, and not thrusting them from their places at feasts. They wanted not likewise a sad preacher at their tables to admonish them daily of death, surely an unnecessary discourse while they banqueted in sepulchres. Whether this were not making too much of death, as tending to assuefaction, some reason there were to doubt, but certain it is that such practices would hardly be embraced by our modern gourmands who like not to look on faces of *morta*, or be elbowed by mummies.

Photographs are our mummies, I think, or were when they had material form, the dead wrapped up in silver nitrate or the common fixer silver halide. It's hard to embrace a digital mummy or be elbowed by one. But just so, when my eyes embraced the sepulchral black lace of the naked dead woman, I was stunned by a wash of nausea that was the chemical assuefaction in my heart. I felt sick, heartsick.

As though she hadn't caused enough trouble, Pandora next gave me a photograph of the woman standing completely naked now, next to a small table in the same room, which I used to call the breakfast nook. She had her legs crossed and her head cocked, lips pursed, a parody of the vamp, vamping nonetheless. She looks somewhere between graceful and strange.

Pandora's box is and was not just about what was inside, what was let loose, like the confused erotic thanatology the photographs shake loose in me but also the box itself, another kind of chamber, another camera. And seeing her in that chamber, I'm reminded of other kinds of magic and one morning in particular. It was spring, and I had woken very early, perhaps 4:00 a.m., before sunrise, though not that much before. It was an unusual time for me to be awake. I wandered down the hall from my bedroom to this small room, which overlooked my little front deck and the oak tree whose branches covered it. When I walked into the little room with the big bay window, I had an immediately strange sensation, something different, something sensually . . . not just strange but estranging. I felt then as though I had a mote in the corner of my eye. And when I turned to the window, I could see, dimly, something large on the branch of the tree. I was very still because I felt I needed to be. When my eyes focused, I could tell, because there was just enough light, that it was an owl sitting on the branch, a barn owl, *Tyto alba* (which curiously translates as "white owl" in Latin). I sank slowly to my knees, trying to will it not to move. It looked like a small haunting spirit, not surprising since barn owls are also sometimes called "ghost owls."

They are also in a category distinct from other owls, strictly nocturnal *Tytonidae*, from the Greek *tuto*, for "owl." Those nocturnal Greeks. Most North American owls are *Strigidae*, typical. The barn owl's face is heart shaped, though slightly elongated, as though the heart were being stretched. So, we have a little winged heart ghost, appearing only under cover of darkness. I wonder if the barn owl was the inspiration for cupid.

But the barn owl also has associations with death. In an old favorite piece of music of mine, Leoš Janáček's sequence for piano and small chamber *On an Overgrown Path*, the composer mixes memories, some wistful but others rather distraught, especially of his twenty-one-year-old daughter Olga's sickness with typhoid. The young woman died.

But she lingered on for awhile, and it was then that her parents clung to hope, "Sýček neodletěl"! This, the title of the most melancholy of the series, means "The Barn Owl Has Not Yet Flown Away." In Czech and other mythologies the flying away of the *Tyto alba* is a harbinger of death, and if the owl sits and does not fly, there is still hope.

But as I said, the girl died.

I watched the heart ghost, the creature of what was left of the night for . . . I don't know how long. It seemed outsized and mysterious to me. Despite my technical posture of supplicant (because of it? what was I asking for?), I blinked, and it flew swiftly into the black grass to kill something and fly away, its extended wings like a warning to not breathe for a moment, both me and the prey. And then it was gone. The barn owl had flown away.

In this essay I can't bring myself to say the dead woman's name, my sense of projected decorum. Though I can also imagine her saying, in her sugared accent, "Oh, honey, I couldn't care less. Just don't show it to Daddy."

Do you remember the myth of Pandora? There are several versions. In the most commonly cited, from Hesiod's *Works and Days*, Zeus commands the Gods to create Pandora after Prometheus has stolen fire. They variously gave her both gifts, attributes such as grace from Aphrodite but also the painful complexities of language and shame, thanks to Hermes, and so on. And there was a container, a *pithos*, really more like a jar but we call it a "box," and so it has formed in our mythos. In the jar were disease and burden, toil and pain, but strangely also hope, which, after Pandora had opened the box, was the one thing that stayed in the box. This has confused some people. Emily Dickinson writes:

"Hope" is the thing with feathers—
That perches in the soul—
And sings the tune without the words—

Like an owl? Does hope stay in the box because of its feathers, because of what it might kill or how it might leave? Must one keep it close lidded? Hope, one supposes, is the only thing that can kill hope—allowing the feeling out of the box only to see it fall, its wings clipped. I'm thinking of the wonderful title of the book of prose by Woody Allen *Without Feathers*, a witty take on Dickinson.

But what is in my boxes is not hope or even the detritus of hope but memory. And I think that's what Pandora let loose upon the world, the myth a clear precedent for the Genesis story, as we bit into, open the top of, see what we're told to stay away from: ourselves and the shadows of our pasts, the recesses we shouldn't linger in, think too much about. Bite that apple, open that jar, at your own risk and see how your garden grows, how hopeful you remain. Paradise is, after all, blissful self-ignorance. Makes sense to me. Pandora, you wrecker of the complacent world.

Pandora is frequently painted as a lovely naked or semi-naked young woman, in the paintings by Jules Joseph Lefebvre, Ernest Normand, Paul Gariot, Thomas Benjamin Kennington, John William Waterhouse, and many others. They're onto, I think, Pandora's melancholy allure. "For she was the muse. You never fuck the muse," Gerald Stern writes in "Lillian Harvey." "How old did she look? Was she like her photograph?" I did fuck the muse before she was the muse, but now I'm just left with a photograph of Pandora herself. Which the dead woman, who by the way loved me very much—I do have to say it, hopelessly—would have smiled about generously, ruefully, because she was very smart, before telling me to pour her another drink.

What does reaching in where we haven't gone forever get us? Sometimes we see things we don't expect. And we're never quite the same again. We just hope against hope to keep a lid on both what we've lost and what we've found.

TO THE READER,
SINCERELY

TO THE READER, SINCERELY

Non men che saver, dubbiar m'aggrada.

—DANTE, *INFERNO* XI

For it is myself that I portray.

—MONTAIGNE, "TO THE READER"

Come here often?

We've both been around the block a few times. In fact, I think I may have even seen you loitering in my back pages. I don't hold it against you. It's like the old joke: we're both here, after all. My apologies if that sounds slightly salacious. But just as Montaigne wished he could appear naked and worried that he'd be cast into the boudoir, it's that desire to be raw and that need to cook, wanting to blurt out everything and wanting, too, to be discreet, that creates the maddeningly necessary friction for essays. It's that thinking about what you think you thought. Raw rarely wins.

I want something from you, and you want something from me, and I'm not just trying to be chivalrous when I say I know I owe you a good time, in the broadest sense. What I want from you is more complicated, reader. You're mostly doing a great job of giving me what I need just by being you. I know that sounds hackneyed: "Just be yourself." And of course, to a certain extent, you're my invention, whether you like it or not, the monster to my Franken-stein—or "steen," depending on my mood. *Potato, potahto.* But if we call the whole thing off, we must part. Keeping all of this in mind, I think it's fair to say you can read me like a book. But even as I'm imagining you, you're (with a little help) imagining me. Which is to say, dearie, old pal of mine, that the thing about whistling in the dark is "You just put your lips together and blow."

Reader, I divorced her. And she me. And perhaps I'm looking for a surro-gate, a perfect other, perchance at least a friendly friend to while away the hours conversing with. After all, I spend so much time talking to myself, writing little concertos of prose in my head, that after a time, having spent too much time walking around the city and thinking in concentric loops, layering idea upon idea only to have them evaporate like the lightest of brain soufflés, it seems to make sense to write them down. I try to tell myself that the story I tell is real, but really, what would that really mean, other than that I really mean what I say? Nevertheless, I think, I've always thought, that intention counts for something. Isn't that recherché? Wasn't intention nine-tenths of the law in some places?

I'm sincere, in other words. Whether or not I'm honest is a judgment that shouldn't be self-administered. I'm sincerely sincere. I've always loved the song in *Bye Bye Birdie* "Honestly Sincere":

If what you feel is true
Really feel it you
Make them feel it too
Write this down now
You gotta be sincere
Honestly sincere
Man, you gotta be sincere.

If I didn't have a dash of modesty, I'd be entirely and wholly sincere! I'm even sincere about the things I say that are slightly less than sincere but which I try to sincerely slap myself around a bit for having been insincere about. It's one of the ways I can show you that I'm being reasonably honest. It's also a sincere display of how flawed I am. Look, if I told you I was thirty-nine and then told you I was fifty (don't roll your eyes), you'd think I was a bit of an idiot, but at least you'd know I had a self-correcting mechanism. But I'd take everything I say with a grain of salt if I were you. And I mean that sincerely. I'm fifty-nine, by the way. You could look it up.

If I really just wanted you to like me, I'd tell you a story. It would be a story of adversity of some kind, and I would be the protagonist. It would arc like crazy, like Laurence Sterne on Ritalin, and I'd learn something really valuable from my experience. But who knows where an essay is going to go? Really. I'd be a defective essayist if all I did was tell stories. Sincere stories. Like the one about walking out of my house yesterday. I was feeling my age as summer bled into fall on a day that was really too nice for such a metaphor. A guy who was working on installing a new wrought iron fence outside (I love wrought iron—partly because I love the way it looks and partly because of *wrought*) told me he liked my style. "Thanks!" I said, thinking I was so smart to have bought that 1950s vintage jacket online last week for fifteen dollars. Then the fine fellow said, "You look like Woody Allen."

I was taken aback. I had never been told I looked like Woody Allen. I'm not sure I want to look like Woody Allen. I don't mind sounding a bit like Woody Allen. It comes with the territory—Brooklyn Jewish—and he was an enormous influence on me. But *look*? So, I said, "I'm sorry, did you say I looked like Errol Flynn?" And he said, "Yeah, that's right but not from *The Adventures of Robin Hood* but from *The Modern Adventures of Casanova*, in 1952, when he was dissolute."

I made that last part up. Forgive me? He really did say I looked like Woody Allen.

For the last few years everyone I've met has been telling me I look like Lou Reed. I don't see it. I was in one of my favorite bars in Chicago, the Berghoff (essay product placement), and a man was staring at me. He finally made his way to my table and said, "Excuse me, I don't mean to bother you, but are you Lou Reed?" I said, "No, I'm John Cale." He said, "Who's John Cale?" I mean, how can you possibly know who Lou Reed is without knowing who John Cale is? It's like walking up to someone and saying, "Are you Oliver Hardy?" "No, I'm Stan Laurel." "Who's Stan Laurel?"

In any case I wasn't even sure of how I felt about that. Lou Reed was great looking, although a bit older than I; he was getting a bit weathered . . . and do I have to look like a Jewish New Yorker in the arts? What's the connection between Woody Allen and Lou Reed? Who's next? Mandy Patinkin? Harvey Fierstein? Hey, what about Adam Brody?

Look, reader, I'm sincerely not trying to look for things to complain about, but part of bedecking myself is the confusion and profusion of identities that *I* shuffles through. Surely you have some version of this? Don't you have some walk-in closet of self or selves? I do have some version of a Fierstein shirt, a Patinkin suit, I suppose, especially when I'm being shticky. When my persona is shticky. When it's less so, I like to think I'm closer to

Me and my shadow
Strolling down the avenue
Oh, me and my shadow
Knock on the door is anybody there
Just me and my shadow.

You might call me a self-made man. Hello to the essay Lazar, good-bye to the talker-walker Lazar. The former has inscribed the latter, imbibed the latter, put him through a meat grinder, and feasted. I'm self-immolated, a phoenix. Rise, he said. Or Monty Python: I write rings around myself, logically, if not impetuously. (Don't you wish John Cleese had written essays?) The spirit of Whitman is in the essay: we enlarge ourselves even as we're talking about our pettiness, our drawers, our moths, our doors. The *I* that takes us along (remember that terrible song "Take Me Along"?—bad songs stay as long as delightful ones) does so because we're attracted to the way it vibrates or concentrates, clicks or skiffles. The essay voice is a boat that can carry two.

And no voices are alike—my own jumpy, interruptive style, which might not be to everyone's taste, will be seen as a flaw or a defect by some and by others as the only dress in my closet. But let me tell you that I think that I, like most essayists, want to be known. That this "created" voice you're hearing (created voice, creative writing, creature of the night!), this persona, this act of self-homage and self-revelation, occasionally revulsion, frequently inquisition or even interdiction, actually is tied very closely to the author. Since I'm frequently my subject, to say the *I* who is writing isn't quite me is slightly fatuous; which *I* is the more sincere, the more honest self? That one? The ontology of essay writing involves a conversation with oneself, and one, after a while, exchanges parts back and forth so that writer and subject become bound, bidden, not interchangeable but certainly changeable. I become what I've created and want to be known as that.

For Montaigne the wanting to be known was partly due to the loss of his soul mate, Étienne de La Boétie. At one point Montaigne offers to deliver his essays in person. I like that idea, reader. We've lost the telegram, after all. Wouldn't you like to open the door and have Mary Cappello or Lia Purpura hand you a personalized essay? "Essay, ma'am," might just enter the lexicon. I'd write you one. I could come over and read this one to you if you like. Like Montaigne, I think I'm in search of company, and I talk to myself in essays as a way of finding it. So, you're really very close to me. A matchbook length, a cough, a double-take away.

At the end of his invocation "To the Reader," his introduction to his *Essais*, in 1580, Montaigne bids farewell. It's a double joke. He's saying good-bye because, in an extension of the modesty topos, he has urged the reader to not read his vain book of the self, his new form: the essay. He is also bidding adieu to the pre-essayed Montaigne, the one who isn't self-created, self-speculated, strewn into words and reassembled, if so. A playful gauntlet. And he is invoking the spirit of his death. To write oneself is to write oneself right out of the world. It's the autothanatological moment: "When they have lost me, as soon they must, they may here find some traces of my quality and humor."

Montaigne says his goal is "domestic and private," and so it may have been at first, though Montaigne's literary ambitions start seeming more and more clear as the essays lengthen and grow more complex, as Montaigne takes more risks with what he offers of himself. And my own, I ask myself, in the spirit of Montaigne. What are they? I'd say they're twofold: (1) to write the sentence whose echo doesn't come back; (2) to be known, in some essential way, without sucking the air out of the mysterium.

Montaigne's address to the reader occurred when doing so was still a relatively new, a reasonably young, rhetorical move. According to Eric Auerbach, Dante seems to have been the first writer to establish an intimately direct poetic address to the reader. Dante then plays with this form, using it as a structuring device, tossing off asides. And Montaigne quotes Dante in the essays. This dynamism is epistolary, liberating, and seductive. Sotto voce. Let me whisper in your ear. It's just the two of us. Come on, you can tell me. Or rather, it's okay, I can tell you. The confession. After all, I'm writing about myself, and my subject is really important, right?

Except: reader, she says—grabbing me by the shoulders, telling me that what she needs to tell me is more important than anything that's ever been told—I married him. And you thought *comedies* ended in marriage? In my triad of great addresses to the reader (meaning me, in the place where you are now), Charlotte Brontë's direct address will always be for me the most stunning, the single most relational, moment perhaps in literature. "Reader." And for the moment it's your name. *Call me Reader.* And as a male reader, and as a male adolescent reader, my response was always: you should have waited for me.

Addresses to the reader are not, you see, just about intimacy. They're also secretly about infidelity.

Reader, comrade, essay-seeking fool, blunderer upon anthologies for whom the book tolls, when I said, "I divorced her," I'm sorry for the lack of context, but really what I wanted to talk about here wasn't her and me, that was a bit of a feint, but you and me. You know I've been missing you. Since we last met, across a crowded essay, I've really been thinking about nothing but you. Well, you and me, and me and you. Let's go for a little walk, shall we? Flaneur and flaneuse or flaneur and flaneur. I might even let you get in a word or two.

Baudelaire must have breathed Montaigne. And his "Au Lecteur," or "To the Reader" (also the title of Montaigne's invocation), is almost like Montaigne inverted, Montaigne through the looking glass. Actually, Baudelaire and Charles Dodgson were contemporaries, which makes a kind of perverse sense. If you look at some of the language, some of the phrasing of "Au Lecteur," you find a Montaignian sensibility, if not a Montaignian tone: "In repugnant things we discover charms"; "Our souls have not enough boldness"; "Our sins are obstinate, our repentance is faint." But whereas Montaigne is only suggesting, via a modesty trope, that his readers may be wasting their time (not really), Baudelaire is saying (hey, you!) we're going to hell in a *panier à main*, which means, ironically, that we need to listen to his brotherly jeremiad. "Hypocrite reader, my brother, my double"—the antithesis and the brother (and sister) of Montaigne's and Brontë's addresses. Theirs are seductive in their close (reading), one-on-one asides to us, just us. They need an intimate, we feel, and so appeal to our need for intimacy. We need what they need. But so does Baudelaire because who else would dare say that to us? Hey, you! Yeah, I'm talking to you! I remember being shocked by that, the audacity, someone daring to say that to me. He would have to . . . know me pretty well. My brother, my double? Push, pull.

Depending on my mood, I could tell you that there are better things to do than reading essays—going for a walk, watching a movie, throwing a rubber ball against a stoop. But at other times, perhaps when I'm treading across Charles Lamb's "A Bachelor's Complaint of the Behavior of Married People" or Eliza Haywood's *The Female Spectator*, Nancy Mairs's "On Not Liking Sex" or John Earle's *Microcosmographie*, I feel like telling you that there may not be anything better to do, that in fact you're wasting your time reading novels or going to plays, looking at art (I can't ever speak against the movies—I just can't), or doing the things you do to keep yourself alive. You should just read essays and live on the delight. The delight of Stevenson, Beerbohm, M. F. K. Fisher. But modesty tropes are worthwhile, so part of me wants to tell you: "Go for a walk."

So, reader. Reader. Darling reader. There's something I want to tell you. It's a story, but it's more than a story. It's what I think about what's happened to me. To us. And where I might be headed. We might be headed. It involves movies, books, walking around if it's not miserably cold, and your occasional willingness to laugh at my jokes. Together, we might be able to cobble together an essay. We can assay! I'd love it if you really thought you knew me.

BEING A
BOY-MAN

The *toga virilis* never sate gracefully on his shoulders.
The impressions of infancy had burnt into him,
and he resented the impertinence of manhood.

—CHARLES LAMB, "A CHARACTER OF THE LATE ELIA"

AROUND FATHER'S DAY, 2013

An ex-girlfriend used to call me her lesbian boyfriend, and this used to please me, flatter me. I felt it gave me the aura of transcending my gender, which, I must say, was, is, much to be desired. Because, after all, who wants to be a "man"? The qualities I associate with manhood I experience in the ways I imagine the descendants of slaveholders feel—shame mixed with disgust. What are these qualities? Condescension, argumentation, arrogance, smugness, entitlement to power, discomfort with powerful feelings. Though gay masculinity has to some extent redefined manhood, slowly, in the larger culture, when I hear the word *man*, a kind of monolith with a penis appears in my mind, with graying temples. I'm Jewish, so the graying temples make sense.

My father was powerful, scary, charming. My mother was warm, accepting, scary. My dog was diffident. I became a kind of gender patchwork: confused, heterosexual, feminized, feminist, inconsistent, wounded, queer. Yes, I know the last is a minefield, fraught, territorial. But it evolved out of a sense of strangeness and difference, and so did I.

When I was a boy, I thought manhood was a prize the Wizard would give me, one of the secret medals he had hidden in his bag. Here is my song to be sung to the tune of "If I Only Had a Brain":

When a boy is wracked and worried
He gets so awful hurried
He's tight as a tin can
Still I'd know life were easy
And I wouldn't be so queasy
If I only were a man.
You know, I need to grow
Right out of the bonds that seem so slow
Life is happening outside of my window
Accelerate! How great!
If you think that boyhood's pleasant
A charming adolescent
Engagement in the show.
I can't bear my position
It's my sole and dear ambition
To stop being young and grow.

But the Wizard didn't give me my manhood medal.

And years passed, and I became a kind of a man by default. First I ran toward manhood, and I've spent the last few decades running away from it. Because, in my way of thinking: who wants to be a man? I'll say more about this. There is the stage in which males in our culture are neither men nor boys, which we call "young manhood." I've actually never heard this noun form alluded to in anything other than the singular form, but someone must have. This stage of being men with training wheels. It might also be called "Late" or "Old Boyhood," but we don't do this because at this stage most

American males are yearning to throw off the shackles of adolescence. *Old Boy* also has connotations that make it more than slightly distasteful.

I think I liked being a young man. *Man* was modified. *Man* should always be modified in my opinion.

If someone, an interstellar visitor say, were to ask me what I am, I doubt I would say I am a man. What would the situation, the conversation, the unfortunate event, be in which I *would* say I was a man? A hospital admittance? A date? Pulled over by a cop? A cop who was a man, no doubt. You were speeding? Gender? And what would be the response of someone to this announcement, to saying, perhaps peremptorily, "I'm a man!" (Are you in a football stadium? Is the ballet about to begin? Giselle?)

Here are some possibilities:

A woman: I'm sorry.

A man: What's it like?

A transgendered person: Are you sure?

A police officer: Proof of insurance.

A dog: Woof.

As a young man, say between the ages of eighteen and twenty-five, I felt sophisticated beyond my years thanks to far-flung travel and the mourning and melancholy that accompanied my still young years of intense introspection, full of unidentified yearning . . . I was compulsive in ways I couldn't control, which scared me constantly, and completely confused about whether or not I was attractive or completely sane. The cauldron of my early political radicalism and the second wave of feminism, a kind of insistent desire to resist convention, and, and . . . what to call it? An aversion to certain masculine norms that had seeped into me from an early age: aggression, loudness, insensitivity, indifference or antipathy to intense emotion and self-reflection. I identified these qualities, stereotypically, of course, with masculinity. Along with my politics, and what Hazlitt called "the Spirit of the Age," while sexually heterosexual, I was spiritually and politically engaged with the (here the writer taps the table impatiently) LGBT movement. My own sense of "maleness" or "man-ness" became diffuse, deconstructed over the years.

I'm a boy, I'm a boy
But my ma won't admit it
I'm a boy, I'm a boy
But if I say I am
I get it.

—THE WHO

Yes, I ran and run away from *man*, but I could embrace some version of *boy*, some version of the open, still-evolving biological masculine nomenclature, even if it carried a whiff of Andy Hardy or comic books. Look, I'm not talking about Peter Pan, about clinging to youth. I think of most boys as more emotionally supple than most men. More sensitive. Charles Lamb referred to himself as a "boy-man." I like that.

The truth is I don't often think of my gender, except when I'm thinking about gender. That's patriarchal privilege in disguise. When I do, I think of it as a kind of male-queer construction, painted with feminine outlines. I'd like to define my gender as Fred Astaire, actually, if I were asked. Fluid but focused. Dances alone, however, much of the time.

HYDRA
I'll Be Your Mirror

When I think of hybrids, I think of the Hydra from Jason and the Argonauts. In 1963 I saw my first motion picture at the Albemarle Theater in Brooklyn. When you say the words *motion picture*, you become aware of being "of a certain age." When you say the words *of a certain age*, you start to feel old. I was six, the age my son is now. I remember the Harryhausen Hydra and those skeletons crumbling after him into the water when Jason jumped from the bluff. It didn't seem quite a heroic denouement, but the jump contains a valuable lesson: that's how you bluff death—by strategically retreating, sometimes.

I saw my first musical, *Oliver*, the same year. I also wrote an aborted, paranoid autobiography that was based on the conceit that I was always being blamed for *everything*. While I have no memory whatsoever of the Kennedy assassination or its aftermath, I do remember that Oliver's song to his missing mother, "Where Is Love?" made me so limbically upset that my parents consoled me and then made me sing it every time there were more than two people, including animals, in our living room. They meant well.

I started to write essays when I was working on a PhD in poetry, about twenty-five years ago, in a workshop taught by Phillip Lopate at the University of Houston. Many American essayists began by writing poems. I switched genres, which at the time felt like changing sports, rather than leagues. Some of my friends like to mention that I did the first PhD in nonfiction writing or creative nonfiction, as though I were some kind of generic freedom writer, as opposed to an early entry to Ripley's *Association of Writers & Writing Programs Believe It or Not.*

I finished my degree and spent years getting my own book of essays into print. Ten years after having been the AWP runner-up in nonfiction, it was picked up for the Sightline series at Iowa, an excruciating gap. Although myself has been in high gear, occasionally high dudgeon and not infrequently high anxiety, since it was forced inward by the outward forces of childhood and my early unlovely body, my essays were all different kinds of juggling acts, with different forms and excessive digressions, photographs, vaudeville versions of the self. My book, *The Body of Brooklyn*, didn't add up to a conventional memoir or book of essays. It was some kind of Hydra—but think of those heads from 1963 as more like obscure objects of my own desire to construct an essay persona. Something like Groucho Marx speaking like Cary Grant having just spent the weekend reading Kafka.

In academic creative writing we tend to think of the Big Three Genres like they were automobile companies. Of the three nonfiction is like General Motors, a kind of supergenre, a generic holding company: it's a collection of old genres, emerging genres, and subgenres; pieces of writing that blissfully have no accurate or legitimate genre to adhere to; and the periodical press. Nonfiction is in many ways a non-genre, the un-genre. Do we need to be liberated from generic pedagogy in the same way that some English departments were liberated from periodicity, not avoiding periods ("Oh let not time deceive you / You cannot conquer time") but not being so rigidly structured by them? They only pay me to ask the questions. Which is why I write essays and why I continue to believe that the essay is the ultimate hybrid—or if you will, *Hydra*—form. I think it might be great fun to have departments of creative writing in which the degree offered was based on Jason and the Argonauts.

Literature has been using hybrid forms at least since Menippus (which sounds like "Not since Ninevah"—from *Kismet*), in the third century BCE, prose and poetry in letters and prosimetra, satires, and plays, a dialogical and indecorous impulse that, as Peter Dronke points out in *Verse with Prose from Petronius to Dante*, "often takes the form of undermining the sureness of authorities, institutions, and points of view, just as, linguistically, of undermining an established decorum of genres and diction." To an extent almost all nonfiction offers some form of hybridity, biographies straying into history, essays digressing into informational riffs, autobiographies becoming necessarily biographical, etc. But nonfiction seems to be at a combinational focal point now, with the lyric essay, graphic nonfiction, "autofictional writing," the video essay, and the relentlessly interesting ways nonfiction literature and film are generically conjugating. It's a great time for Hydras.

Nevertheless, part of the current fascination with combined forms is, I think, born of ignorance, of how central and intrinsic these forms have always been to nonfiction. Think Augustine, Seneca, Addison and Steele, Keats's or Millay's *Letters* or Kafka's *Diary*. In the furthest corners of nonfiction we find an endless array of forms bridging disciplines, bending rules: Harry Stack Sullivan's *The Psychiatric Interview* or Georg Groddeck's *Book of the It*, Georg Christoph Lichtenberg's *Waste Books* or Elizabeth David's recipe books, Joe Brainard's deadpan "I Remember" memory aphorisms or Anna Kavan's autobiographical novel, *Sleep Has His House*. Kavan, for those of you who don't know, was the name of Helen Ferguson, who changed her name to the name of her fictional character, Anna Kavan. Nonfiction sometimes seems like a Sea of Cognates, which sounds as though it's just past the Hill of Difficulty or the House Beautiful. There are those works of nonfiction that engage in more than one kind of nonfiction writing and those that cross genres, bring together prose poetry and poetry, like the books of poetry that proliferated after Hass's early books or the fiction and essays in Primo Levi's *The Periodic Table* or in almost all of Jacques Roubaud's work (the French, who are a funny race, and especially the Oulipolians, are much less fraught about genre issues, having been liberated by Rabelais and the *nouvelle roman* centuries and minutes before 1963), or see genre as a playground or smorgasbord: Annie Ernaux, Patrick Modiano, Georges Perec, as do Eduardo Galeano, Jorge Luis Borges, Wayne Koestenbaum. The French also lack the equivalent word for *nonfiction*.

The personal essay or classical essay (even these terms are problematic—I prefer *essay*) is hybridic almost by definition: its middle or conversational or familiar style shuttles between colloquial and formal dictions like a crosstown train. It is a free and plastic form, "unmethodical" in Lane Kauffmann's now oft-quoted phrase. But last week I heard an essay complaining that it had been inviting in guests, poets, fiction writers, writers of ill repute, all of whose company the essay enjoyed but some of whom wanted the essay to change her name. "You other genres, I bend myself backward for *you*," the essay complained, "and what do I get? You still want to hyphenate me or change my name." She was an essay from Gravesend, and she wasn't taking any shit. The essay may tarry with other genres, but does it really need to marry them?

Try this. In his book *Objects and Empathy* Arthur Saltzman writes of the lyric essay: "It is ruminative, sly, self-effacing, intimate, sneaky fast, and (as long as we're breaking in new expressions) 'idiosyncretic.' Instead of final findings, it provides an adventure for the voice and the self's invention." This sounds indistinguishable from the personal or classical essay. Or if we must subgenerate, might we say that lyrical and personal essays overlap in ways that haven't been theoretically distinguished?

Is Montaigne a lyric essayist, in his sometimes elusive, elliptical, or concentric style? Or is he too discursive, standing out in the rain of explication? Benjamin in "One Way Street"?—the essay as architecture of urban memory, essay as series of arcades. *The Pensées*: a set of lyric essays as extended aphorism. And where do aphorisms and lyric essays meet or separate? Cioran, Nietzsche, etc.? Weil? Lyric essay as hyperextended prayer, as theological maze. As series of aphorism? Burton? Lyric essay as cabinet of wonders. As medicine cabinet. I usually think *lyrical* should be adjectival, the "lyrical essay," rather than subgeneric noun. These questions interest and annoy me, depending upon the day and hour. But I also wonder whether *lyric essay* is another equivalent of *creative nonfiction*, reflecting an unnecessary anxiety about the genre the way the dreadful *creative* does and is hitching the essay to a ride with poetry so it can go creative writing–legit (psst, it's a fugitive genre) or because the market for nonfiction is perceived as growing.

Plus, every time I hear *lyric essay*, I think of Rodgers and Hart. The Great American Essay Book. My funny Emerson. Sweet comic Emerson. You make me smile with your transcendental insights. Although what Stanley Cavell calls his counter empirism is attractive in places and close to the worldview of some lyrical essays. But my associations with the word *lyric* are indelible. 1963. Brill Building Essays. "It's My Essay and I'll Cry if I Want To?"

When I've taught the essay, I've always encouraged hybridity, telling my students that the essence of the essay is, as Lukács and Adorno have remarked, its formal openness, that we can write poetry in our essays (or prose in poetry, for that matter, as another way of considering an essay), like Fred Astaire turning a stroll into dance in *The Band Wagon* or Judy Garland coming out with "The Trolley Song"—let me be a little more hip: like André 3000 singing "Life Is like a Musical" in *Idlewild*—that students can essay in blocks, in paragraphs, in lines, in any typographical form, wrapped around photographs, scribbled in margins of old comic books. The essence of the musical is the need to switch rhetorical gears, to intensify, to lyricize through song and dance. And perhaps my interest in hybrid forms stems from my early love of musicals, that Great American Hybrid Form. Think of *Singin' in the Rain*: it's a history of film, a parody, a love story; it's got a long fantasy sequence with a film noir element; and it has a variety of dance and musical styles, etc. The show within a show, as Rick Altman, in his crucial book of theory *The American Film Musical*, points out, is a familiar musical motif, allowing for disjunction, friction. Gotta essay?

But the lyric essay is also literary history catching up with nonfiction, the postmodern era of the essay, full of untrammeled and self-conscious experimentation. It's a market correction to the excesses of slovenly, untheorized autobiographical writing, a tonic to soggy memory writing, to bad autobiographical essays that perhaps were never really essays at all. In that sense there's a kind of irony in the notion of any tension between the lyric and the personal essay. Nevertheless, temporarily, sincerity seems out of favor because sentimentality crept in. Parataxis is in, and syntax is out. But the lyric essay at its best reminds us of how poetic a form the essay can be and always has been. The work of Lia Purpura, Thalia Field, Etel Adnan, Jalal

Toufic, D. J. Waldie, Sir Thomas Browne, Colette, Virginia Woolf, reminds us of how the essay can move and think most lyrically. But that's not all these essays do.

On the other hand, essays that gesture with pale motions of ironic self-regard or stay safely within the generic confines of circumscribed selves do little for the form or its readers. You know who you are.

Essays inevitably need to change rhetorical gears and create new rules as they go. But at what point does an essay need to be nominally qualified or modified generically? Is the essay's hybridity sufficiently intrinsic for us to think about questioning subgeneric overdrive? The lyric essay, the braided essay, the fractured essay, the meditative essay, the fragmented essay, the sad clown essay, the skim latte essay, the hey-look-me-over essay, and of course, last week's special, the This-Is-Not-an-Essay essay. The essay does so many things, invokes so many, that trying to name it every time it does something new, contains a long obituary, or reflects Barthes/Sontag by using photographs or meditates with a different kind of proximate distant to the self, as in Colette Brooks's wonderful *In the City*, we're tempted to see a new genre, as opposed to an expansion of our sense of the genre. It's a measure of the success of the essay recently, I think. Call it genre-fication. Everyone wants a piece of the action. I'm from Brooklyn; we write Fucking A Essays. Sometimes they change gears right here so they can talk about two hybrid works that I love.

Let's make a lyrical jump to the Gawannis, where I once saw the car ahead of my parents' hit a dog and the dog went spinning around on the road at night. I went back to sleep in the back of the car because it was so sad and scary, and my father said, "Fuck." My mother said, "Leo!"

My mother's name was Rhoda, and I wanted a transition to talk about a book by Dhuoda, the *r* dropped for a *d*, my first initial and *hu*. It's a hybrid work by a Carolingian woman of the ninth century, written to the son she'll never see again. I didn't realize for about a month after uncovering my fascination with *Liber manualis* (*A Handbook for William*) that having written a book, more or less for Rhoda, I was obsessed with a book written for a son a thousand years ago by Dhuoda. For someone who has tried so hard so often to be the good little analysand, this was disquieting. Pretty slick, huh?

Gloria Anzaldúa is the mother of contemporary heterogeneity in Menippean poetic-prose form.

Maxine Hong Kingston is the mother of contemporary nonfiction in imaginative narrative literature.

Gertrude Stein is the mother of some versions of the lyric essay.

As you can see, for me, other than Montaigne, mothers are where the action is.

Dhuoda's husband, William of Septimania, sent her off after she bore him a son. She didn't see her husband for sixteen years, after which he visited her, conjugally, and the resulting son was taken away from her. Her first son, William, was sent by his father to be used as a hostage, proof of his loyalty to Charles the Bald. This is a heartbreaking story—not a Marx Brothers movie. To console and instruct her son, Dhuoda wrote *The Handbook for William.* Dhuoda's text opens with:

Here begins text.

The little book before you branches out in three directions. Read it through and, by the end, you will understand what I mean. I would like it to be called three things at once, as befits its contents—rule, model, and handbook. These terms all mirror each other.

Dhuoda writes a mirror, a genre called a "speculum"; hers is a hybrid form full of prose advice, literary criticism, lyrical admonition, quoted psalms and poems. Book 10 is penultimate, blending poetry and prose, hope and despair—chapter 1, "On the age you have attained":

And if in twice as many years and half again
I were to see your image,
I would write to you of more difficult things, and in more words.

But because the time of my parting hastens,
And the suffering of pains everywhere wears my body down,
I have in haste gathered this book for your benefit and your brother's.

Dhuoda follows this with a chapter "On the verses I have begun with the letters of your name," an acrostic in which she writes:

And so my noble son, seek diligently.
Take care to hasten to receive
Such great rewards, and turn away your eyes
      From the fires of blackened wood.

The image burns more than the instruction instructs. Chapter 3 is a short postscript on public life, in prose, followed by an epitaph in verse. Book 11 follows with more brief advice. The good mother, no doubt, doesn't want to leave her speculum with her death.

Is the spirit of Menippus alive in Dhuoda, a work everywhere preaching paternal forbearance, allegiance? Is there a hybrid imp in the author of this work, also known as a *liber manualis*? Well, no amount of modesty topoi can sweep away these lines, from book 1, chapter 2, "On seeking God":

It is absolutely necessary for me to do so in all things. For it often happens that an insistent little bitch, scrambling under the master's table with the male puppies, is able to snatch up and eat such crumbs as fall. He who makes the mouth of a dumb beast to speak and opens my understanding, giving me insight according to his ancient mercy, is indeed a powerful Lord.

These moments, these inconsistencies, of form, of self-presentation, are precisely what create this specific Dhuoda and her mirror, this anxious *mater dolorosa*. I think of the yearning in Nico's song "I'll Be Your Mirror" when I read her. And I think of another hybrid form, another speculum, written a thousand years later, by Elizabeth Smart, also trying to essay a new way of articulating love, anxiety, desire, pain.

Smart's *By Grand Central Station I Sat Down and Wept*, which I blundered across when I was living in England twenty years ago—between giving up on my degree in poetry and Phillip Lopate convincing me to return to Houston and finish my degree in prose—and happened to read her obituary, came into print finally a few years ago in the United States and just as quickly went out. Her book of extended prose poetry, fractured narrative, mythological invective, and urban descant is too hot, too purple, too masochistic, for some still fifty years after it was first published in England and Canada. Here are the last few lines, written to a conflation of lover and unborn child; if they don't make you long to read the rest, you shouldn't: "Yes, it's all over. No regrets. No postmortems. You must adjust yourself to conditions as they are, that's all. You have to learn to be adaptable. I myself prefer Boulder Dam to Chartres Cathedral. I prefer dogs to children. I prefer corncobs to the genitals of the male. Everything's hotsy-totsy, dandy, everything's ok. It's in the bag. It can't miss. My dear, my darling, do you hear me where you sleep?" Smart is among the few writers I know who appears to risk everything, to be emotionally raw, formally wild and self-aware, yet lucid, lucid. It's hard to imagine Jeannette Winterson without her in some way, even though they're so tonally different, these breaks with form, these songs of the body. In *By Grand Central Station I Sat Down and Wept* Elizabeth Smart's love affair with George Barker, a minor British poet with whom she fell in love and eventually bore four children sans marriage, Barker's guilt-ridden return to his wife and subsequent illness after he and Smart are arrested on morals charges in Arizona, and Smart's tormented meanderings alone, carrying their first child, are the narrative features upon which the lyrical hyperbole of the book is based. Smart's book is part roman à clef, part interior dialogue between reason and amour fou, part prose poem in language that stretches the limits of poeticized despair to the brink of and sometimes beyond the breaking point. It's somewhere between Hazlitt's *Libor Amoris* and Duras's *The Lover*: purgatorial, obsessive, extravagantly self-involved, lit up in language that threatens to self-destruct as its figurative formulas alternate between the biblical and mythological, folding metamorphosis into metamorphosis, with the occasional intrusion of modern urban diction and imagery and flares of ironic despair. Eliot's influence is everywhere, but there is no mythic method to lead one out of the blind alleys of Smart's emotional labyrinth. In the literature of anguish it belongs in the pantheon.

In the beginning of part 4, reimagining her arrest with Barker on a Hayes Act charge, Smart counterpoints the intrusive and absurd questions of the Arizona State Police with lines from the *Song of Songs*:

What relation is this man to you? (My beloved is mine and I am his.
He feedeth among the lilies.)
Did intercourse take place? (I sat down under his shadow with great
delight and his fruit was sweet to my taste.)

A few pages later she implores, "My love, my dove, undefiled, go into the telephone box with Diogenes and dial a number that someone will understand." We might call this imaginatively transfigured narrative.

At times Smart's world turns Gothic, a demonized landscape with wildly personified emotions haunting the houses of Nature and Bad Faith, her inherited tabernacle and bordello, neither of which offers a comfort sufficient to relieve or release her from guilt and obsession. Smart wanders between the two, just barely skirting the Slough of Despond, variations of which abound: "the sand of catastrophe," "the cliff of vigil," love's pilgrim in a world whose helpers are all sorry evangelists of easy moralism. We're back to Bunyan, to whom Smart is clearly in thrall.

If this sounds busy and exaggerated, it is. *By Grand Central Station* approaches at times a kind of mad and maddening miasma in which Smart, the "continually vibrating I" in her terms (a Montaignian phrase if there ever was one), glimpses what she is in the grips of. But this ferocious voice of midcentury can toss a gauntlet, a grenade of unexpected prose, at the conventions of autobiography and essay while still locked in the grips of amour fou to the end. *By Grand Central Station I Sat Down and Wept* is the *Wuthering Heights* of nonfiction, neither perfectly essay, autobiography, nor memoir. The imp of perverse Menippean genre breaking peering through the window of our conventions, Smart challenges our existing categories of genre. Poetic memoir? Occasionally epistolary book-length autobiographical prose poem? Perhaps, though unwieldy. Extended allegorical essay. Allegorical essay? Oh, no . . . Perhaps essay-novel, to accompany Sebald and

Kundera. In any case it's a hybrid form, lyrical to its core, on a cellular level, and deeply personal.

I once wrote an essay on *North by Northwest,* a film in which Cary Grant is the same age as his mother, played by the essential Jessie Royce Landis. Hitchcock's wish fulfillment? The essay was a critical-personal-lyrical braided essay with some poetry. And a cherry on top. It was an essay.

A hybrid word is etymologically divided and united, its constituents coming from different languages. I hate the fact that 9/11 sentimentalized Auden's "All I have is a voice / To undo the folded lie," from "Sept. 1, 1939," because I used to use it to talk about the essay. I can't anymore. But in Tom Stoppard's *The Invention of Love* A. E. Housman says: "Homosexuality? What barbarity! It's half Greek and half Latin." Homos latched on to sexus. Leave it to Stoppard, who's always breaking rules. Let's think of ourselves as trans-genred. Who wouldn't want to write that?

A CONVERSATION WITH
ROBERT BURTON, AUTHOR OF
ANATOMY OF MELANCHOLY (1621),
VOX ES, PRAETEREA NIHIL

DAVID LAZAR: Some of our readers might say they wouldn't be caught dead reading a thousand-page, seventeenth-century compendium of quotation, essay, digression, and aphorism about the state of our incorporeal infirmities. What might you say to such a reader?

ROBERT BURTON: Now go and brag of thy present happiness, whosoever thou art, brag of thy temperature, of thy good parts, insult, triumph, and boast; thou seest in what a brittle state thou art, how soon thou mayest be dejected, how many several ways, by bad diet, bad air, a small loss, a little sorrow or discontent, an ague, etc.; how many sudden accidents may procure thy ruin, what a small tenure of happiness thou hast in this life, how weak and silly a creature thou art.

DL: Thanks. I'm sure Amazon sales have now reached the torrid zone. Considering the intensity of your achievement, your influence on Johnson, Sterne, Lamb, Keats, so many others, does the fact that you are so little read sting you at all?

RB: A modest man, one that hath grace, a generous spirit, tender of his reputation, will be deeply wounded, and so grievously affected with it, that
he had rather give myriads of crowns, lose his life, than suffer the least
defamation of honour or blot in his good name. And if so be that he cannot
avoid it, as a nightingale . . . dies for shame if another bird sing better, he
languisheth and pineth away in the anguish of his spirit.

DL: It's good to hear such a balanced perspective. Within *The Anatomy of
Melancholy* are some of the great essays in the English language, the "Digression of Air" ("what God did before the world was made? was He idle?"),
"Artificial Allurements." Can you speak to the way you assay, how you
crafted these bold, wandering Montaignian essays in your swift, barely
post-Elizabethan prose?

RB: One must needs scratch where it itches. I was not a little offended with
this malady, shall I say my mistress Melancholy, my Egeria, or my malus
genius, and for that cause, as he that is stung with a scorpion, I would expel
clavum clavo, comfort one sorrow with another, idleness with idleness, *ut ex
vipera theracum* [as an antidote out of a serpent's venom] make an antidote
out of that which was the prime cause of my disease.

DL: So, you're saying that writing is therapeutic? Many writing professors
reject that idea.

RB: Cardan professeth he wrote his book *De Consolatione* after his son's death,
to comfort himself; so did Tully write of the same subject with like intent
after his daughter's departure, if it be his at least, or some impostor's put
out in his name, which Lipsius probably suspects. Concerning myself, I
can peradventure affirm with Marius in Sallust, "That which others hear
or read of, I felt and practiced myself; they get their knowledge by books,
I mine by melancholizing."

I am of Catullus's opinion and make the same apology in mine own
behalf: I write for the most part to satisfy the taste and judgment of others; I
am not mad myself, but I follow those who are. Yet grant that this shows me

mad; we have all raved once. And you yourself, I think, dote sometimes, and he, and he, and of course I too . . . howsoever my lines err, my life is honest.

DL: Point well-taken, and I see you've read my work.

RB: I have not offended your chaster ears with anything that is here written, as many French and Italian authors in their modern language of late have done?

DL: I'm from Brooklyn. Moving on. Do you have any new projects planned?

RB: Give me but a little leave, and I will set before your eyes in brief a stipend, vast, infinite ocean of incredible madness and folly: a sea full of shelves and rocks, sands, gulfs, euripes and contrary tides, full of fearful monster, uncouth shapes, roaring waves, tempests, and siren calms, halcyonian seas, unspeakable misery, such comedies and tragedies, such absurd and ridiculous, feral and lamentable fits, that I know not whether they are more to be pitied or derided, or may be believed, but that we daily see the same still practiced in our days, fresh examples, *nova novitia*, fresh objects of misery and madness in this kind that are still represented to us, abroad, at home, in the midst of us, in our bosoms.

DL: Sounds great. Almost like Anatomy II. There was a rumor floating around that you hanged yourself. Comment?

RB: *Corpora cito extinguuntur.*

DL: Isn't that a somewhat coy response?

RB: Do you wish to be freed from doubt? do you desire to escape uncertainty?

MEET MONTAIGNE!
(WITH PATRICK MADDEN)

On a pleasant afternoon outside Bordeaux, in his tower at the corner of his family château, the writer and statesman Michel de Montaigne, stocky and bedraggled in britches and poofy blouse, was serving us wine from the estate's northerly vineyards.

"I speak my mind freely on all things, even those which perhaps exceed my capacity and which I by no means hold to be within my jurisdiction," he assured us as he wandered to a shelf and began fidgeting with a book of Cicero's poems. "I set forth notions that are human and my own, simply as human notions considered in themselves, not as determined and decreed by heavenly ordinance . . . as children set forth their essays to be instructed, not to instruct."

The beloved former mayor and advisor to French kings is perhaps best known for his three-volume collection, *Essays,* which he began writing upon his retirement in 1572, at the age of thirty-seven, when he discovered that simply allowing himself idle time to read and think led his mind, "like a runaway horse, [to] give itself a hundred times more trouble than it took for others, and [to] give birth to so many chimeras and fantastic monsters, one after another, without order or purpose," that he began to write in order to "make [his] mind ashamed of itself."

His first two volumes of *Essays*, which appeared in 1580, contained this prefatory warning: "Reader, I am myself the matter of my book; you would be unreasonable to spend your leisure on so frivolous and vain a subject." Yet readers did spend their leisure on reading the *Essays*, enjoying Montaigne's candor, his wavering even-handedness, his playful, associative mind on display in the text. And not only in France in the sixteenth century but around the world and through the centuries.

This simple man of letters seems as surprised as anyone that his literary legacy has lasted over four hundred years. "I do not love myself so indiscriminately, nor am I so attached and wedded to myself, that I cannot distinguish and consider myself apart, as I do a neighbor or a tree," he commented as he poured refills, then tenderly passed us an original printing of his book. "Here you have some excrements of an aged mind," he chuckled, "now hard, now loose, and always undigested." And we all had a hearty laugh together.

PERSONAL

Born February 28, 1533, in Guyenne, France. Married to Françoise de la Chassaigne (1565–92), with six children, one who survived infancy.

WHY YOU KNOW HIM

In his *Essays* Michel performs acrobatic mental feats of association, considering everything that comes into his purview with artless art and graceless grace. "It is the language of conversation transferred to a book," said Emerson. "Cut these words, and they would bleed."

What you don't know

Out of respect for her honor, I have never gazed upon the breasts of Mme de Montaigne.

I will not sit with thirteen at the table. I can dine without a tablecloth but very uncomfortably without a clean napkin. My teeth . . . have always been exceedingly good . . . Since boyhood I learned to rub them on my napkin, both on waking up and before and after meals. I am not excessively fond of either salads or fruits, except melons.

My meat: rare.

Favorite movies?

I was expecting more, or perhaps less, from *Stoic*. Perhaps the prison film is not my genre. *The Cannibals* was interesting in a lurid way, surprising in its Sophoclean inspiration. I frankly thought there would be more about the cannibals. Perhaps I'm too literal about these things. *A Man for All Seasons* was one I watched several times. It reminded me that as an ill conscience fills us with fear, so a good one gives us greater confidence and assurance.

When I dance, I dance, when I sleep, I sleep, and I think Fred Astaire is like a sleep dancer, walking on air . . . that magical man. He seems to stop time. So, I'd say *Swing Time* is a good one, with Ginger Rogers . . . I am very much driven by beauty. So, let's just say anything with Rita Hayworth. The felicity that glitters in virtue shines throughout all her avenues and ways. Oh, and "Put the Blame on Mame"!

What books are on your nightstand these days?

I study myself more than any other subject.

Understood, but any books grabbing you lately?

Erasmus, Rabelais, La Boétie . . .

What do you think of more contemporary essayists, say, James Baldwin?

If you press me to say why I loved him, I can say no more than because he was he and I was I. I also quite like that fellow Sebald.

We understand that your tastes in music run from des Prez and Willaert to more contemporary fare. Can you share with us some of your favorite popular songs?

"Boys, Boys, Boys" by Lady Gaga would seem to capture the essence of the Socratic impulse. Then there's "I Just Don't Know What to Do with Myself" by the White Stripes. Lisa Hannigan's "I Don't Know" is quite good. Dusty Springfield sang a song very true to my way of thinking, "How Can I Be Sure?" Then, of course, Ray Charles singing "You Don't Know Me" speaks to me of the wavering and noncommittal natures we carry in this shifting world. Similarly, the Clash's "Should I Stay or Should I Go" comes from a dilemma I have often found myself contemplating.

So, this new book After Montaigne. . . *what do you think of the use of your work as the basis for new musings?*

I seek in books only to give myself pleasure by honest amusement. I seek only the learning that treats of the knowledge of myself. [*After Montaigne*] has this notable advantage for my humor, that the knowledge I seek is there treated in detached pieces that do not demand the obligation of long labor, of which I am incapable.

I find it admirable at representing to the life the movements of the soul and the state of our characters. I cannot read it so often as not to find in it some new beauty and grace.

Amongst so many borrowed things, I am glad if I can steal one, disguising and altering it for some new service. All the glory that I aspire to in my life is to have lived it tranquilly. There is nothing that poisons a man so much as flattery.

But I'm flattered.

THE TYPOLOGIES OF
JOHN EARLE

Typification is the process by which we create categories of types, divisions, and classifications based on similarities. Typological constructions exist in almost all disciplines: theology and psychology, anthropology and linguistics. There are formal, named typological systems such as Blanchard's Transsexualism Typology, which sought to create a variety of categories, much criticized, of transsexual experience. The Oakeshott Typology is a classification of medieval sword, broad or flat, long and short, pointed or dull, etc. . . . . The Sasang Typology is a classification scheme in traditional Korean medicine. People are divided into four types: greater yin (Tae-Eum) and lesser yin (So-Eum) and greater yang (Tae-Yang) and lesser yang (So-Yang). Tae Yang have large lungs but apparently a liver that is quite small and a tendency to suffer from inferiority. Tae-Eum, on the other hand, have a liver that is quite large but, alas, lungs that are below par. They tend to be tall but portly, and though persistent, they are prone to gambling. I'm trying to think how many Tae-Eums I've known. I'm not Tae-Eum, of course, because I'm on the small side and do not gamble. I'd like to think of myself as So-Eum, large kidneys, skinny, intestines a bit weak, some digestive problems . . . but that may be because I like saying, "So-Eum." It would be nice to walk up to people and say, "I'm So-Eum."

The point is we have all kinds of ways of putting things in categories. It's a way of reducing the overflow of information and making sense of the world. There's the old joke "There are two types of people" that everyone has been riffing on since God or Satan gave us binaries. Binaries are essentially just another form of typology, a typology of opposites. Good and evil, start listing who and what goes into each category, so we can make clear distinctions. What violates and expands categories, typologies, even if creates more complicated typologies, makes people nervous (think Hannah Arendt) because it means we have to think more, that distinctions require more work.

A phrase that I found popping up all the time in my lexicon in the last few years is *The thing is*. When I say, "The thing is," I'm creating a category, a typology, of what I think is essential. The thing is that 90 percent of what people love about the arts in America comes out Vaudeville." The thing is that Henry Adams was just Henry James with a political pedigree. These might be categorical statements in a loose sense, but they're what Kant would call "hypothetical imperatives," something I say that I have to do something about, to know more or to prove, again in a loose sense. Typologically, this puts me in the class of speculative thinker and writer who is conventionally called an "essayist."

And I think that in the essay much of what we do is both create and resist typologies, perform an inner and outer dialectic between our desire to narrow the possibilities and understand things better and the desire to not narrow them too much, to keep them open, in fact. And in consequence.

Early in the history of the essay, this convergence of typification and exploration, so essential to the essay's nature, comes together in the largely forgotten work of John Earle, whose ecclesiastical life and career in some ways run parallel to Montaigne. Earle was born on the cusp of the seventeenth century, 1601, just nine years after the death of Montaigne, six years after Marie de Gournay's final version of the essays. This means his birth antecedes the first short enterprise of the English essay, *Bacon's Essayes: Religious Meditations, Places of Perswasion and Disswasion, Seene and Allowed*, by four years. The much larger second and third editions of Bacon's *Essays* come in

1612 and 1625, the latter when Earle would have been a fellow at Merton, the College of Scholars at Oxford.

Earle moved his way up the ecclesiastical ladder and must have had some clear ambition for such, having been appointed, variously, as chaplain to the earl of Pembroke, chancellor of Oxford, chancellor of Salisbury Cathedral, chaplain to the future Charles II, bishop of Worcester, and dean of Westminster. He was a royalist, a loyalist, but by all accounts a moderate. He was a friend of Izaak Walton, who in his *Life of Hooker* describes Bishop Earle's innocent wisdom and sanctified learning, "a clergyman, despite his successes, of rather modest, even disinterested attire," described by Lord Clarendon in his memoirs and others as being witty, "facetious," modest, though critically keen; he sounds almost like a churchified Lamb two hundred years avant.

The only work, other than translations, that he left us is the strange, quirky, funny, essayistic, occasionally cranky book of short typographical essays, *Microcosmography, Or, A Piece of the World Discovered*, first published anonymously in 1628 by Edward Blount, one of the partners in the printing of Shakespeare's *First Folio*. It proved so popular that it went through ten editions in Earle's life (he died of the plague in 1665). But it wasn't until the thirteenth printing of the book, in 1732, that John Earle received attribution as its author. He had been long buried at Merton College, Oxford.

Microcosmography is a strange and delightful book. In it Earle sketches out types of characters, such as "A young raw preacher," "A grave divine," "A plausible man," "An idle man," "A sordid rich man," specific micro-types of human character that can be read through physiognomy and action but whose inner condition Earle speaks to also. He also creates broader categories, of profession, for example: "A surgeon," "A baker," "A cook," "An attorney." And his third broad category, containing the fewest entries, are of place: "A prison," "A bowl alley," "A tavern."

Earle is a moralist and an ironist—he can't help finding foibles, poking fun, seeing the way we do things based on what we have become or how we have become things—preachers, say, perhaps even bishops—based on who we have been. In that sense there is the light air of determinism in his sketches, as there tends to be in any typology, I think. If we are going to fall into a category, it's probably going to be well-groomed, for us and by us.

But I'm interested most in the form and the style of Earle, as I tend to find much of mid- to late English Renaissance prose delightful. The history of the essay in the seventeenth century is curious, to say the least, beginning on the cusp, with Bacon's parentage of the English essay as a distinctly more aphoristic, less personable, tightly screwed and self-corked version than his predecessor, Montaigne.

The best English essayists of the post-Elizabethan period, interestingly, are somewhere between Bacon and Montaigne—more Montaignian in style perhaps, looser, less aphoristic, more fanciful, than Bacon. But they frequently write a short version of the essay that has little to do with Montaigne's historical and philosophical meandering. It's as though they took the charm of Montaigne, the length of Bacon's essays (anywhere from a couple to, say, five or six pages in contemporary terms) and Bacon's more narrow focus, if not his taciturnity, and created yet a new path, or really several, since each of them is practicing a variation. So it is with a new form. And theirs, really, on some level would determine the direction of the English essay and what we consider the personal essay for centuries. I am speaking now of essayists such as Cowley, Fuller, Temple, the strange essay works of Burton, which are virtually new forms entirely, and perhaps Locke, whose essays breathe more than Bacon's but are less interesting to read (we don't sense the repressed personality, the intensity, the neuroticism, that creeps in between the lines of Bacon) as well as others whose work adds to the growing corpus of essay.

It is the overt quirkiness, the idiosyncrasy of voice, of personality, that becomes the dominant motif in the English essay, and here we can draw a line distinctly from Montaigne to Cowley and Burton, Addison and Steele, Sterne, Lamb, to Geoff Dyer and Jenny Diski, etc. . . . Hazlitt writes, in "On the Disadvantages of Intellectual Superiority," "Now I hate my style to be known, as I hate all idiosyncrasy," sounding a theme that Orwell would pick up in "Why I Write." And in some ways Hazlitt acts as a corrective to essayistic whimsy and authorial peculiarity; he frequently dazzles through *argumentative* idiosyncrasy and complexity, rather than that of voice. This is to say his subject is less often himself. Personality, after all, expressed in style, which is what we call "voice," does not by itself create an essay. But Hazlitt also protests too much, undoubtedly because of the accusations of his own peculiarity. He has more than his share of idiosyncratic moments.

The typology of essayists, and I'm not going to produce one, though I think it might be fun to at some point, would certainly include as one of its largest categories those writers whose sensibilities were finely attuned and somewhat skewed. In other words, the idiosyncratic in the essay has probably been the norm, and the attraction for the reader has been the identification with a point of view relieved of the banal, the familiar. If essayists frequently consider the quotidian, the close at hand, they do so by defamiliarizing it; they're canny and uncanny.

To return to John Earle, consider what he says in the opening sentence of his "Acquaintance": "Is the first draught of a friend, whom we must lay down oft thus, as the foul copy, before we can write him perfect and true: for from hence, as from a probation, men take a degree in our respect, till at last they wholly possess us: for acquaintance is the hoard, and friendship the pair chosen out of it; by which at last we begin to impropriate and inclose to ourselves what before lay in common with others."

This makes me want to teach a class entirely devoted to the long sentence. John Earle, Montaigne, Melville, Henry James, Virginia Woolf, James Agee, Samuel Beckett . . . This sentence itself: Earle leads us through multiple possibilities of acquaintanceship, as trial or apprenticeship of friendship, which is a form of possession. Twice in the sentence Bishop Earle suggests acquaintance as the common form, the public form, the "hoard," to the internalized, private, select friend. But Earle also suggests that acquaintance is practice for friendship, even though it is often a "foul copy"—and here his language suggests the dangers perhaps of both life in the ecclesiastical and court chambers and our more common need to try to figure if someone is really who they seem. "I know not seems," Hamlet says to Gertrude, about the possibility of pretense, but to get to the truth of things he has to know "seems," both in himself and others.

Earle goes on to stress the idea that acquaintance has its place as a lesser good, the fancy to friendship's imagination: "Nothing easier than to create acquaintance . . . whearas friendship, like children, is ingendered by a more inward mixture . . . when we are acquainted not with their virtues only, but their faults, their passions, their fears, their shame." Here, as in many or most essays, it is really his desire to talk about friendship, the deeper subject, that takes over, since it haunts, in an extraordinarily felicitous phrase, the "verenda of the soul" and allows us the chance to share "those things which we dare not shew the world." Earle goes on to allow that when we travel, acquaintance may be convenient. But like love, which has been the subtext, as it is for Montaigne, Earle suggests that if it doesn't take at first, it won't ever: "Men that grow strange after acquaintance, seldom piece together again." All the king's horses can't make a friend if our experience is "disrelishing." But if it were relishing, good bishop? Yes, we understand, that would be an acquaintance picked from the hoard to cherish.

In "A Surgeon" Earle shows himself sharp and sensitive, snarky and heady, writing close to the body and indulging in what sounds like eighteenth-century wit. This piece, barely a page, would make an interesting counterpoint to Richard Selzer's brilliant essay "The Knife," written 350 years later, the surgeon in Selzer much elevated from the hack who hopes for injuries in Earle. But true to essay form, Earle's piece is full of internal friction, the surgeon who "deals most with broken commodities" and "complains of the decay of valour . . . and sighs for that slashing age of sword" because it "wound[s] his profession," but he is clearly the repairer, the fix-it man of the body, the blue-collar medic—that is why the metaphor of the building trades repeats. Moreover, as in any of the trades, he is forced to earn a buck, which the good bishop never had to do but is aware always of everyone else having to do. The surgeon looks to the tavern for windfalls—brawls from broken heads. He's a necessary evil, a pain in the ass, only to be trusted in the performance of his specific duties, if in that. That sounds like the soul of Bacon, though Earle's springs are wound less tight.

In his place pieces Earle is a moralist and seems to love the general hoi polloi while, as always, being a flaneur of the action: he never gets involved.

No Bishop bowling. There are all kinds of *types* here: gamesters, gamesters' beadsmen (praying for bowlers!), gamblers, losers. Earle writes, "It is the best discovery of humours, especially in the losers, where you have fine variety of impatience, whilst some fret, some rail, some swear, and others more ridiculously comfort themselves with philosophy." It's a sweaty, shilly, place full of high and low, base motives, "bodies into such strange flexures." This is, in other words, a place much like the bowling alleys I grew up with in Brooklyn. It's also a space that sounds very much like the essay to me: embodied, open to philosophy, even if absurd, in the realm of "the mistress fortune." And as such it is, in its narrow confines, "the best sport" and "the best discovery of humours." Earle was speaking of bowling, I mean: the essay. Six of one.

VOLUPTUOUSLY, EXPANSIVELY, HISTORICALLY, CONTRADICTORILY

Essaying the Interview with
David Lazar and Mary Cappello

MARY CAPPELLO: You open your new collection of essays with a wonderfully suggestive epigraph from Terence: "That is true wisdom, to know how to alter one's mind when occasion demands it." Of course the word *occasion* and *occasional* function in variously meditative ways in your collection, and I don't want this question to serve as a spoiler, but I was curious to hear your thoughts on the difference between being what used to be known (and maybe still is) as an "occasional poet" and how the idea of the occasion(al) figures (differently) for you in these essays or in the history of the essay. Mainly, I'm struck by the way the Terrence epigraph might speak to the utter adaptability of the essay form and therefore—here's my question—of the essayist? What might that mean for you?

DAVID LAZAR: Thanks for this question, Mary, because it's rather central for me. The occasional poet, say in the laureate sense (Larkin turned down the laureateship because, among other things, he couldn't imagine writing "occasional poems") hews to an event, current or celebrated, of public import. The poem may veer to more personal moments, but it's essentially a public form, and its themes shoot larger rather than smaller. The occasion in the essay is frequently quite different. Certainly, large themes and events may come into play. One hopes they do. But more often than not, essayists are moved to write by events, ideas, problems, questions, coincidences, conundrums . . . that are smaller and closer to home. Because the voice in the essay is so often intimate, we like to know fairly early on why it is the essayist is writing the essay, what brought her here, in short what the "occasion" of the essay is, what stirred her to write. And I divide the occasion into two crude categories, "ostensible" and "actual." The actual occasion might be there right from the beginning, upfront. But it also might be discovered; it might be hidden from us, the way dreamwork hides our deeper anxieties, and the "ostensible" occasion, which got us writing, allowed us to wade in to where we needed to go to find our "real," or at least more necessary, subject. So, this is a partial response to my invocation of Terence. The other part is simply the necessity of being able to think and change one's mind while writing an essay. In fact, it's impossible to write essays without being able to do this. Let me go further: I can't imagine wanting to write essays unless this is an essential part of your makeup: the desire to change something in yourself, to move it off the mark, unsettle it. When I begin an essay, I have a rough idea of the subject and the occasion (the two might merge or overlap) and perhaps a few things I think I might want to say at some point, some pieces of narrative I think might be useful. But then when writing, I might find that the essay needs to be broken up in a certain way (which I do very selectively) or that my original idea was just a hedge or that some of the thoughts at the beginning of the essay were timid and that I need to go much further or that they were reckless and I need to pull back. If you look at the Montaignian essay or the Hazlittian essay, you find coils of intensity. Part of my resistance to the subgeneric categorization of the essay (segmented essay, ekphrastic essay [aren't all essays ekphrastic?], lyric essay), in addition to the fact that they're just academic inventions of creative writing programs that are mimicking the academic development of poetry, is that it stifles the ability of students to do what they most need to do: allow their minds to voluptuously, expansively, historically, and contradictorily develop a sense of what they might say in an essay and then figure out how to write stunning sentences to speak them. The second part is hard to teach. I mean, you can always do forms.

Let me add that where the occasion is concerned, you and I both seem to be perennially taken by, swept up a bit by, intensities of coincidence. In fact, we met under auspiciously coincidental circumstances, you writing to me before we'd ever met on the morning after I had ordered your book *Awkward: A Detour*. So, you return to what I might call "the frisson of circumstance" a lot. Why do you think we do this, Mary? Is it just that we're these meaning-making machines without much spiritual guidance, speaking for myself, so when we bump into people we know in Oshkosh or the number 72 repeats itself on an excessive number of billboards or we meet a woman with the same name as our childhood crushes, we have find something in it? Accident becomes a kind of inscrutable and necessary principle? Oh, one more thing: I had just reread what you wrote about the bezoar in your newest book, *Swallow: Foreign Bodies, Their Ingestion, Inspiration, and the Curious Doctor Who Extracted Them*, and I was walking down the street with Delmore (my son) and he started spontaneously talking about bezoars. What are the odds?

MC: Hmmm . . . let me riff a little on *occasion* with you first. I hear you saying that the occasion is the spur, ground, impetus, maybe the essay's condition of possibility. Or what used to be called its "inspiration" but less grand, more ordinary. That the occasion changes—it needn't be adhered to; it can be left behind: like the flame's starter, it's easily evaporated. Stevens maybe concurs with you when he writes: "The poem is the cry of its occasion / Part of the res itself and not about it." Maybe the essay's occasion is akin to what Freud calls the dream's navel—the place where it originates but that is ever out of view and can't be gotten to the bottom of . . . it's what compels and propels the writing but remains outside the realm of interpretability.

David, you got me going to the OED, where I discover that Occasio is the Roman equivalent of the Greek personification of opportunity, Caerus or Kaerus, and both are represented—I love this—as having a long forelock at the front of the head while bald at the back of the head. Which sort of makes *occasion* punk. Apparently, the idea was that opportunity is fleeting, so you're supposed to grab it while you can; if you miss it, you're left grasping at nothingness.

Somewhere the word *occidere* figures in its etymology as well—that the occasion is that which falls, without befalling one: I mean it's a kind of happy accident. To essay might require that one give oneself more fully over to chance and might explain our shared penchant for coincidence: I think it has to do with a willingness to make oneself susceptible, to stay open to being found by a subject rather than go in search of one. Like all good concepts, it's really polyvalent. For me the draw of coincidence is its kinship with synchronicity and simultaneity rather than diachronicity or linearity. It's the contradiction of all that happens side by side that interests me more than causes and their effects.

At the same time, sure, I think that we're drawn to coincidence as a way of dealing with our own traumas: it's a way of protecting oneself from loss and chaos. (I wrote about this in an essay called "Shadows in the Garden" on the various forms of grief modeled to me by my Italian American family.) Our aptitude for coincidence helps us to feel surprised and consoled simultaneously. I think it makes the world less lonely seeming: it says, "The feeling is mutual." Coincidences as mutualities. I suppose they're in the realm of what I call "weird shit": they're interruptions that also seal things up. Of course, as a perceptual mode, what we're talking about also treads a fine line between delusional thinking and metaphor making.

A most beautiful and uncanny meditation on coincidence is Lawrence Weschler's *Everything That Rises: A Book of Convergences*, which I'm sure you know. And what you're saying about the failure of our essayistic categories might resonate with Michael Theune's *Structure and Surprise: Engaging Poetic Turns*, in which he proposes an alternative to the age-old taxonomies of poetic forms.

I remember the first time I read the title essay of your collection, "Occasional Desire," in your anthology *The Truth in Nonfiction*. I was so grateful for the way you were asking me *to think* about the essay and the friction between desire and memory therein, the way that desire challenges memory's narrative complacencies, as you might put it; and I was grateful for your willingness to historicize current practices so nimbly and instructively—you put it so succinctly when you suggest an essayist needs literary knowledge and knowledge of the world. I got hooked on your work starting with this essay on the essay, and then, when I read the title essay in your *Body of Brooklyn*, I felt haunted by the places it was willing to go—really into realms we might consider taboo, some dark underside of things, of life, and yet what were you dealing with but the place we all live but don't want to admit into language or consciousness. You were writing, in particular, about being a boy who had been fat or who had been thin and attendant sexual anxieties and identifications, including identifications with the feminine. I wondered if you might talk about what feels like a psychoanalytic logic that shapes some of your work (I'm thinking especially of the essay on "Dating" in the new collection). Drawing upon some of your own compelling poles and zones, how do you gauge the difference between "I and one" in your work? Between "solitary confinement and writerly solidarity"? Between "self-knowing and self-analysis"?

DL: Hey, stop being so interesting. Oh, I know, you can't help it. Now, wait a minute, protecting ourselves from loss and trauma? Did I get off at the wrong bus stop? I know what you mean, our always failing attempts at trying. I'm always alluding to Freud's navel too. Images of the master on a Viennese sunscape. To be serious: in what gets us started, some subconscious sense of more dangerous, yes, opportunities. It's like going for a walk and not avoiding the chasms in your path. You need to fall into them. And then you need to get out. Finding them, falling, and getting out are where an essay's living quality survives. I'm speaking of a certain kind of essay, of course—the essay where self-understanding is highlighted in some way, which tends to be the kind of essay I write—what I call a very psychodynamic process for the most part. As for taboo, yes, it's important for me to "speak the thing that shouldn't be spoken about" from time to time. Don't you think that's thrilling? Don't you think that's fun? Don't you find your ten-year-old self sitting in the corner waiting for your mom to find out? Part of me writes against the family injunction not to speak outside the family and simply to not be afraid to say things. As in: there, that wasn't so bad, was it?

To respond to your last few questions: we all spend a lot of time stuck in our heads, and we think all kinds of crazy things. I experience my own sense of self, I think—what I also call "sensibility," which is a word I'd like to hear you muse about—very intensely, sometimes pleasurably, and often burdensomely. Part of the sport of writing essays, and the great essayists— Woolf, Baldwin, Hazlitt, Chesterton, etc.—all knew this, is how and when to generalize. One can't be afraid to make a general statement about the world, to try to assume that many others feel the way that one does. By the same token, you're also frequently expressing an individual, personal, even at times a neurotic point of view about the world or some small piece of it. In addition, we have sensibilities (and here I feel my Jamesian side itching to come out) that want to come out and dance around the room and show off their bright affectations with all due condescension (I'm channeling James). So, I've used four different pronouns in the last four sentences. And the first person wasn't necessarily the one in a most personal voice. Nor do I think it should be eschewed. The difference between pronouns is all in the tone, the ballast of context. You can have a warm *one* or a cold *I*. Let me tell you (he says in his best Brooklyn accent).

I do think when I am speaking to myself in the essays you refer to, it's never, and this is a severe issue for me, just for the sake of my own self-analysis. The idea of that makes me queasy. What makes essay writing so difficult is the razor edge between what we consider "truth" in some form—the search for it, honesty's *machine*—and performance, theatricality, craft, poetry, persona, revision. I use my self-analysis to try to get to something beyond myself. In the "On Dating" essay I wanted to use myself as a kind of factotum for the way we construct narrative. And ask the readers to think about how self-serving they are. I tried to seduce the reader with amusement before pulling the carpet out from under myself. I don't know if it worked. As fascinating as I am, I want my readers to ultimately think about other things. That may be the difference between an autobiographical essayist and a familiar essayist. I'm not sure I've answered your questions. I must lie down. The chaise. Quick, bring me the chaise. Or a folding chair.

Better. As a plug, I did want to mention that I'm a Lawrence Weschler fan too. *Everything That Rises: A Book of Convergences* and *Mr. Wilson's Cabinet of Wonders.*

One of the haunting things about *Swallow* is the idea of epistemogenesis that you . . . bring up. "Desire and knowledge are forever linked." Yes, *desire* for me is one of the sacred words, and I mean desire in all its nuances. The book itself performs the function of taking in and bringing forth. And one of our oldest stories (epistemo*genesis?*) is about eating what we're not supposed to eat. But you bring out the centrality of mouth and throat. It's a polymorphous book! And I felt a little afraid after reading it, as though I were going to swallow something bad. Of course I would have this reaction. Did you find yourself checking your plate to make sure it was safe? Did all this work make you more self-conscious about your apparatus, or has it blissfully faded?

MC: You say conundrums, I say conundra, but as we know from one of our favorite musicals, difference fuels desire rather than cancels it. I never said I was interested in Freud's navel. If I were asked to think about Freud's body, it's his jaw that would interest me most and the painful fact that the inventor of the talking cure had to insert and remove a prosthetic device in order to talk, the result of a horrible cancer of the jaw and attendant surgeries.

As for interest, it's a subject I'm very much interested in. I mean, I'm not any more interesting than the next person, but I am interested. I've been wanting to write a collection of essays on the subject of interest—and aversion—and love, inspired by a number of post-*Swallow* encounters and friendships, uncanny discoveries, and yes, more serendipities. These range from being found unexpectedly by the daughter of a boy whose unusually ghastly case study I deal with in the book and the circumstances of that connection; to discovering medical films and home movies in the home of [Dr. Chevalier] Jackson's great-grandson; to being given a tour of the cemetery he is buried in in a hearse by a historian who is also a funeral director there; to finding a ninety-three-year-old woman who worked in his clinics as a voice pathologist who lives in a retirement home with the mother of a friend of mine and who enjoyed a second career as an experimental writer; to being contacted by a woman who was bequeathed the clinic demonstration doll: the story of the medical mannequin, named "Michelle," and its maker and the uses to which she was put could yield a book in itself.

Essayists, I think, at any rate, are people who are interested.

I'm intrigued by the image you invoke of essaying as a chasm we fall into and have to find our way out of. I don't find myself trying to get out of the chasms when I write; I think I'm trying to invent a new way of being inside of the chasm. I'm not sure I ever get out; the writing is just a different way of moving around à la *Barthes* by Barthes: "Writing is that play by which I turn around as well as I can in a narrow place: I am wedged in, I struggle between the hysteria necessary to write and the image-repertoire which oversees, controls, purifies, banalizes, codifies, corrects, imposes the focus (and the vision) of a social communication."

Your earlier set of adverbs says it all, I think—I'd love to adopt them as an adverbial mantra for essaying: "voluptuously, expansively, historically, and contradictorily." They remind me that the sort of nonfiction we're hoping to teach and write is neither disposable nor a means to an end nor a way of filling time (as in airplane reading): it's a writing that incites a new way of being in time.

Where *sensibility* is concerned, I don't take the term to be equivalent to personality or idiosyncrasies or the ego's flourishes and therefore the thing we might want, à la Eliot, to escape when we write. The cultivation of a sensibility is to my mind a lifelong pursuit, and it's not reducible to style per se. It's our way of making sense out of sentience, the place where our being both sensate and sense-making creatures meets. It has an ethical dimension; it treats writing as a response-ability by which we might come to feel thoughts and think feelings. In my classes I oppose the cultivation of a sensibility with a notion students may have that a writing class can give them a bag of tricks, or how-tos, to take away with them. Instead, I try to foster an atmosphere for helping them to cultivate a sensibility.

In *Swallow* desire meets knowledge in so many ways: Jackson is such a complexly desiring being and one who contributes vast new forms of knowledge to the history of medicine. Human beings originally come to know the world through our mouths, until we in some sense literally replace the things in our mouths with words-as-things in our mouths. The human swallow is uniquely precarious and dependent upon a suite of voluntary and autonomic movements in sync: the proximity of airway and food way is marvelous and bizarre and vulnerable making (thanks to our descended larynx, an effect of our evolution as bipeds). And the mouth has got to be the place in the body with the most going on: breath, speech, appetite, desire, language, voice.

I don't know if working on *Swallow* made me more self-conscious of the apparatus or fearful of all of the ways it might cease to work, as you point out. My father treated the object world as a constant possible threat—always warning us that we had to be careful not to swallow things—so maybe I was already self-conscious, and the book was my antidote! But Jackson's foreign body collection pointed up the extent to which we are essentially porous. I seem to have a fascination with incorporation and capaciousness—the fundamental question of how the world comes to withstand us and we it (I'm paraphrasing Adam Phillips here). But I'm also interested in things that appear where they're not supposed to (thus, the draw of the incongruousness of foreign bodies in a human gullet). *Swallow* is thus not so far from the preoccupations of *Awkward*: with adaptation, fit, the cockeyed. What happens when we cross thresholds, either via the mixing of literary genres or in real life? Whether I'm a working-class student at a high falutin' college or a lesbian in a heterosexist world, I'm hopeful not to sacrifice all that is alien to a feeling of "home."

I loved your essay on the journey—emotional, physical, literary, spiritual—to meet M. F. K. Fisher. I wonder if we might talk about the pleasures and challenges of following a biographical subject, dead or alive, to the extent we have both done this in our work. The ways in which one is never merely an amanuensis even when one finds oneself taking dictation. I guess if we put M. F. K. Fisher and Chevalier Jackson side by side, we could say we've also both written about "appetite," albeit from very different directions. Speaking of biography, though, I have a biographical question for you: how did you decide to go to Philip Larkin's funeral?

DL: I'll work backward, since working forward is frequently so laborious. Plus, we know where it gets us. More about coincidence and convergence really, Mary. I had been walking around Regents Park memorizing Larkin poems. I would walk from Chalk Farm, where I was living, past Primrose Hill over to the park, each day putting more and more of a poem to mind. "Home Is So Sad," "Talking in Bed," "This Be the Verse," "Aubade." It wasn't my first flush of Larkin. I actually remember where we met. I was seventeen and in the poetry section of the NYU bookstore. And I picked up *The North Ship*. I bought it and then the other slim Faber volumes. In any case he died when I was living there, and there was a little ad in the *Times* (of London) saying if one wanted tickets to his service at Westminster, one should write to the rector. And I thought immediately, "Why would anyone not go to Philip Larkin's service?" I also thought it was pretty strange to have to get a ticket. I mean, as a Jew I've had to deal with the lifelong anomaly of needing a ticket to attend services for the most solemn day of the year. But a funeral ticket was right up there for a listing in The Sacred and the Profane (which I've always thought would be the best ever soap opera title). I've written about the service elsewhere, so I don't want to belabor that, but realizing I was sitting on T. S. Eliot ("teach us to sit still"?) was quite a shock.

I had two other very strange conjunctions that year that have stayed with me. One was that I was reading Elizabeth Smart's *By Grand Central Station*, which someone in London had told me about, and she, too, had died. Smart was quite well-known in London, still not very much in the States, unfortunately, because Grand Central is an astonishing book, a lyrical hybrid decades ahead of its time. Intensely moving, politically messy. I love it. Kind of impossible to categorize. In any case it's been an important book to me. It's very courageous.

And for my third—there must be a third—in this series, I was taking myself on a little weekend holiday to Cornwall, chugging along on the train, and reading Woolf's *Between the Acts* for the first time. One of the things that's marvelous about traveling is how we remember what we've read and where. I read Doris Lessing's *Golden Notebook* in Castelfranco di Sopra in Italy in 1987. I also, strangely enough, remember reading Lessing's *The Summer before the Dark* in Latvia in 1978. I read *Ulysses* in a small Polish café in London in 1986 . . . etc. I was reading *Between the Acts* on my way to my little holiday, and Woolf mentioned this little regional town in, what must it have been, Dorset? Or the edges of Dorset? And I looked up, and I was there. We had stopped, and I was there, at the station of that town. It was the purest experience of the uncanny I've ever had. Because I was reading because I was traveling because I suppose I wanted to be somewhere else, I was. If I had it to do all over again, I would have gotten off the train. But I was very happy. I was in a kind of stunned happiness. But no, it was a bit more delicate than that.

About M. F. K.—thanks, Mary. Yes, we both became interested in rather formidable characters. Both, too, rather escapable in different ways. I think to convey what's fascinating about one's subject, you have to become a little obsessed with them. Now, our cases are different in that you summoned an intense amount of remarkable research into Chevalier Jackson and performed a kind of psychobiography, along with essaying the nature of swallowing as metaphor and giving us surgical history, etc. But it's that drive that keeps right there with you throughout *Swallow*, wondering, what is this guy all about? What makes it doubly interesting, though, for a reader and as a work of nonfiction literature, is that *you* become this intense literary persona, not just some anonymous narrator, so we're also asking, what is this woman all about? Of course, your readers already know that, but I mean for a reader coming to your work, to this book, cold. Then, I think, with a biographical subject, we have to at some point, both in the work and within ourselves, start heading out of the maze. Don't you think?

With M. F. K. Fisher I had offers to do biographical work, and after editing the book on her and writing a bit about her, I figured it was time to look at other things. You don't want to turn into a cottage industry on your subject. I would have started getting bored. No matter how enthralled you are by your subject, there's a bit of burnout. You don't want to be married, after all, to your obsession. It starts to feel oppressive at some point . . . We're generalists, hummingbirds. Do you want to talk about that?

Also, I was really struck by what you wrote about "pica," "untoward hankerings of nature." I love that. And the connection, etymologically, to magpies. Magpie? That would be dessert, I suppose. Especially since the collecting of stray bits of information, the constant taking in of things, seems so much a writer's preoccupation, bordering on a disorder. We're all kind of suffering from pica, don't you think? I think that's where so much of *Swallow*'s fascination comes from.

MC: Travel on foot or by train, movement, convergence, coincidence: it's such a beautiful recipe for essayism, and it reminds me of the work you are doing now in which you write (and photograph) from the position of a flaneur in your city of Chicago. Can that kind of creature still exist in the twenty-first century? You tell me he can and does! I'd love to hear your thoughts on this, and especially as they relate to that other means of transport—the telephone—in the essay "Calling for His Past," which opens your new collection, on (the now largely defunct) public telephone. I was moved by the way the essay was structured—almost like a piece of music—by way of carefully placed and choice snatches of the overheard: from the guy who forces you out of a phone booth with "Say good-bye!" to the mysterious note found in the phone booth, "Phil Abbate keeps calling for his past," and the wonderful line of Mrs. Gitmann, "I love all the fish in the ocean." I think of these moments as poetic distillates that leave you in the very interesting position of a very specific sort of essayist-receiver (telephonic pun intended). This made me wonder how your essaying (or anyone's essaying for that matter) might shift and change given the newer relationship to publicity and privacy since the advent of the portable phone, that only seemingly private "cell." Eavesdropping seems less possible because people have become so indifferent to their being in a public space. Does the essay change once the "public telephone" is no more? Or when the line between the public telephone and the private telephone ceases to exist?

Are we generalist hummingbirds? Thanks for that rich image, David. It got me thinking of the hummingbirds that would arrive at my window this summer, directly next to my writing desk. (I know, it's scarily idyllic, but rest assured, the writing is never easy.) They never hold still for a picture, try as I might to picture them. They dart; they swoop upward and jet stream at odd angles, like Disney's Tinker Bell, and it's anybody's guess whether they are drawn to what's actually inside the flower or simply its color, its form: in that way their moves seem similar to our own. Sometimes, as I'd turn my head to watch one, it would pause and hover and directly face me as if to learn if I might be part geranium or just to give me the briefest encounter with hummingbird consciousness. An essayist is like a hummingbird in the way she moves from flower to flower, but I'd need a different bird for my own aesthetic because I place a high premium on dwelling (which I think is quite different from obsessing, even though the words are synonyms). This is why I'm not so eager to "get out" because I'm convinced that if we stay with a subject long enough and let it overtake us, it can become something else. I guess I'm after a kind of staying not to be confused with miring and more akin to transformation. *Awkward*, as you know, was based on a desire to sit with discomfort and see what becomes available as a result, rather than, in the age of 9/11, move on as quickly as possible from the disaster, forfeiting our capacity to understand it or to respond with care.

Staying with this idea of the essay's movement and the way we move, or pause, in the world, I'd love to see what might happen if writers of essays, reviewers of works of creative nonfiction, and essayists themselves suspended their use of the word *digression* for a while. I find the word utterly meaningless and inadequate to what essayistic *writing* is and does. Consequently, I'd love to hear more about this wondrous phrase you bring to Hazlitt and Lamb, *coils of intensity*. It's also interesting that we have a language for leaps, silences, associations, and appositions in poetry but not in essays, even though this is what essays are also made of. This is one reason why I want to resist *digressive* as a descriptor for what essays do. I feel like we can afford to do better, but that would require our really lovingly attending to essayistic prose in order to find *a language for the shape* of what we're reading and hearing.

Digression is a misnomer because it privileges both a point (as singular vantage and aim) and a center. But essays at their best think like Gertrude Stein, and therein lies their pleasure and their difference—"act so that there is no use in a center," "aim less"—and embrace pointlessness: "I do not write in order to be right."

I think there's a big difference between digressing and wandering. Digression feels neurotic—a Poesque imp of the perverse?—whereas wandering takes courage, and it's also not the same as "changing the subject": it's a staying with the subject that requires that we approach it from numerous different pathways.

The linked essays book I mentioned earlier is, come to think of it, partly propelled by the difference between drifting and digressing. By the power of and difference between trance and daze and by the new relationships that become possible by moving adrift. Relatedly, I don't think of it at all as a sequel to *Swallow* (like a literal p.s.)—that would require that *Swallow* be a blockbuster, which, for better or worse, it certainly is not. I think of the book I want to call "Waylaid by Interest" as a segue: it doesn't follow from the previous book so much as it's a detour suggested by it; it moves out from it and on from it.

I say all this, and yet this is NOT the book I am currently composing. Right now I'm writing a book on mood and atmosphere [*Life Breaks In: A Mood Almanack*], tempted by the idea of a literary form that could approximate cloud formations. But here's where the hummingbird comes in again, I guess, because while I'm working on one book, there are always two or three others calling upon some part of my consciousness but that have to wait, and thus, again, that need for the more patient bird because it requires such immense patience to work on what is before one and all the time that takes, all the while knowing we only get one lifetime and don't have "forever" at our disposal.

Like you with M. F. K. Fisher, I certainly did not wish to spend my life writing a biography of Chevalier Jackson, though the project could have easily demanded that—Jackson was a pack rat who lived to be ninety-three years old. If there is such a thing as a "definitive" biography, I guess *Swallow* could be considered a "suggestive" biography: I followed the paths of the things that Jackson's life and work, his autobiography, case histories, and most especially his cabinet of curiosity—the foreign body collection— suggested to me. But I based my meditations on a great deal of time spent in archives, in reading, interviews I carried out, and research, and I treated the materials I was privy to of his life and work and that of his patients with loving care (the medical case histories of other people I consider, in partic- ular, a form of sacred document). I've written elsewhere of the biography as brick or doorstop, as extended Wikipedia article or attempts to make the mess of a life cohere, over and against another kind of biographical writing, deformed and gangly (à la Montaigne). Jackson himself was onto some- thing when he wanted to orchestrate his autobiography in terms of three categories—"Physique," "Hobbies," and "Episodes"—rather than produce a chronological narrative. Much to the chagrin of his editors, he also shifted between the first and third person (not *one* but *he*). What they really wanted from him was a "success" story that moved simply and seamlessly from here to there, but he was a nonnarrative assembler through and through.

David, are there other biographical subjects who have inspired your interest or whom who are considering writing about since M. F. K. Fisher? And if so, what's the draw of communing with those other lives?

DL: About the phone essay, which I wrote quite a long time ago and then kept taking out for a spin around the dance floor from time to time, to see how the rhythm worked, changing the steps here and there . . . yes, it's much about the "found" world, especially the found aural world. There's a wonderful book by [Elias] Canetti called *Ear Witness* (modeled on Theo- phrastus and La Bruyère) in which he sketches paradigms of character, frequently through bits of "overheard" comments. I like catching the strays . . . but I'm averse to chasing them. I used to know someone who would silence me so she could listen to the conversation at other tables, and it drove me nuts. If I'm going to be the aural equivalent of a voyeur, I don't want to be methodical about it. But that's my own aesthetic of the found. You know, finding that strange encrusted thing on the beach is one thing, but going out with one of those metal detectors is another. I don't want to be one of those over-tanned guys with a high-tech divining rod. Though it might be interesting to talk to one of them. People are talking less to each other, of course, and grunting into their phones more. I just don't think it's an interesting way to live, walking around with earbuds in your ears. I know that's a classically curmudgeonly thing to say, but the city has an aural environment, and I want to hear it when I walk. The aural atomization has affected me as a walker (shades of Alfred Kazin), which is central to my persona, so I feel when I'm walking now as though I'm threading my way through a crowd of the aurally displaced. Or perhaps it's I who is aurally displaced. Always the last to know.

But at least to reassure you about pedestrianism, I do walk, a lot. On a steamy night, the other night, I walked forty-five minutes to my favorite movie theater, the Music Box, the best old revival house in Chicago, for a showing of the restored 35 mm version of *Leave Her to Heaven*, with Gene Tierney. Chicago is a great walking city. For me walking to the movies combines two of my greatest pleasures.

To digress . . . I couldn't resist. I don't think I resist the word *digression* as much as you do. If it has a neurotic association, perhaps that's why I'm fond of it. I'm not sure there's always a pointlessness to the essays I admire by, say, Woolf or Baldwin. Frequently there's a very strong point. And a still, or hot, center. And a necessity to verge away from there because it's so hot (or even cold sometimes) to the safety of the poignant relevance of one's own experience when, say, speaking about a more general issue in, for example, *The Fire Next Time*. Not so safe in that case. As we both know, generalizing about essays is so alluring and dangerous because the form is so alluring and dangerously generous. It lets us think the form could be almost anything. Well, almost, maybe. But in fact I want to completely join with you about the idea that the vocabulary for talking about the essay is under-theorized. So that a word like *digression* becomes an all-purpose word when it can't possibly serve to describe everything we want it to (which doesn't mean, I think, that it's useless). But *wandering* is lovely. And describes something very different. And what we need, what the form needs, are actual practitioners (named Mary Cappello) to write the essay called "The Wandering Essay."

I can't wait to see what you're doing with mood. Speaking of which, I think there are wonderful belletristic essays that do wander a bit as you're describing—something like essay tone poems. Like Ravel or Fauré essays. I think some of Belloc's essays have that quality, even some of Morley's city essays.

And I may have subconsciously stolen the hummingbird metaphor from Henry Miller, who has a strong book of essays (better than his fiction) called *Stand Still like the Hummingbird*. Isn't that a fine title?

About new projects, I am writing about biographical subjects! In fact the new project I'm working on is all about biographical subjects: character actors. Each chapter an essay on a different character actor: Thelma Ritter, Edward Everett Horton, Jessie Royce Landis, Leo G. Carroll, William Demarest, Sydney Greenstreet, Gloria Grahame, Beulah Bondi, Jack Carson, etc. I've always had an intense response to characters who weren't the lead (undoubtedly because that's how I think of myself) who, in the economy of Hollywood film at least were allowed to be quirky and frequently brought that quality from film to film. I may be the only charter member of the Jack Carson fan club. And Horton, for example, who was gay, constructed a very complex masculinity on screen and was also half of my favorite screen marriage: he and Jean Dixon playing Professor Nick Potter and Mrs. Susan Elliott Potter in *Holiday* (1938). The leads, of course, were Katharine Hepburn and Cary Grant.

Speaking of masculinity, Jackson was this very nineteenth-century character in some ways, it seems to me. Part Dickensian (with maybe a splash of Lamb), although he was both Oliver Twist and part Modern Man. I have the sense that Chevalier Jackson was this wounded, obsessive, strange, magical, enigmatic, talented little man. Does his story make you shiver at the strength of determinacy (the poor tormented boy!) or marvel at the possibility that anyone can survive childhood? You lead your reader to a kind of Barthesian meltdown with his boy patient, Michael H. The photograph in the final chapter of *Swallow* is so wounding, so impossible to look at, so impossible to not go back to. It's his sneer of pain to me—I don't know how else to describe it. He seems so individual, the photograph so concentration camp like. In any case I thought it was a really gutsy move so near the end of the book, and then it leaps back to that other boy, the young Chevalier. It's a very poetic swing and an elegiac one.

MC: Thanks, David. The question of "scale" and the giant who was Chevalier Jackson is an interesting one. Not exactly a Napoleon complex kind of guy; I'd say he was a person who was both larger than life and *petit*. His best-selling 1938 autobiography is structured partly according to a rags to (metaphorical) riches determinacy, but I'm just as interested in the fact that we're always dealing with his own account of himself—I mean, it's a version of his life that reflects how he wanted to be pictured, rather late in his career. And I enjoy a kind of dance with him in receiving the invitation to read his life in a particular way and then push it a tad further: the bullied boy grows up to carry out aggressive acts that save people's lives. He cuts off their airway, takes them to the threshold of consciousness—as other boys had done to him as a boy—but brings them back up for air like a gallant knight.

I'm moved by people who achieve degrees of delicacy in their lives in spite of having been victims of routinized violence. He was manhandled as a child; as an adult, he uses his hands with uncommonly exquisite, unerring delicacy. When I happened upon his coat rather late in my treks to the numerous and voluminous archives that house his ephemera, I gasped at how small it was. And it's probably not beside the point that when I saw the coat—draped with that aura of absent presence that always accompanies the clothing of the dead—it occurred to me that it was just my size. I mean, there are always degrees of denied and displaced identification in biographical work, of kinship and estrangement, of possession and dispossession.

I can't wait to see what you do with that fabulous list of character actors (Thelma Ritter in *The Mating Season*: I could watch that performance a thousand times and wish I could memorize her wisecrackingly brilliant one-liners!). Do these characters find us, or do we find them? There is a curious sort of companionship in this kind of work, and I think it's in part what distinguishes nonfiction from fiction: a call for company.

You really get to the bottom of that photo of Michael H. with that phrase *his sneer of pain*. Discovering Michael H. felt nearly mystical: the fact that his case study was left behind in Jackson's barn. That Jackson apparently had set it aside, bestowing some special significance on it. The fact of my going through this last bit of ephemera as an afterthought. And my realizing I'd seen this boy, this case, again and again in terribly anonymous ways in Jackson's textbooks but only now was being found by his story: the actual case history, complete with full name and address, country of origin, and its tragic end. It was a majorly unexpected puzzle piece, the shadow of which had been following me while I was working on the book without my knowing it. The case was a failure, but Jackson was a perfectionist. I wanted to understand the various ways in which the docs who hadn't listened to Michael H. failed him. I'll never forget that feeling: as though I were being visited by the ghost of Michael H., asking, after all these decades, for someone to tell his story. And how it felt like a discovery in two directions: did I find him, or did he find me? It was clear to me that I needed to end the book with him: I wanted him to have the last word.

The "aurally displaced"! Have I told you about my newfound fascination for Margaret Wise Brown, the children's book writer best known for *Goodnight Moon*? I learned about her unexpectedly in Hillel Schwartz's extraordinary nine hundred–page book on "noise." I was teaching a course in what I call "literary acoustics," focused mostly on nineteenth-century American texts (what happens when we read "The Tell-Tale Heart" alongside the contemporaneous invention of the stethoscope? Or if we begin to consider Dickinson's vestibular aesthetics? I frame the semester with a sound walk that the class and I orchestrate on campus). Brown, as it turns out, wrote numerous intriguingly illustrated children's books on noise and sound and silence. And she was queer: she spent a good part of her life in a relationship with the ex-wife of John Barrymore, a poet who called herself Michael Strange. Is it time to get really wacky? I ran into Strange's coat in an exhibit on sartorial dandyism at the Rhode Island School of Design. Sadly, the placard that accompanied the coat made no mention of Strange's relationship to Brown, only of her connection to Barrymore. That coat was also a lot smaller than I imagined it to be. Wouldn't ya know. In Italian there's a slang word for *faggot* that yokes queerness to auricular displacement: gay men are the people with big ears.

You've written an essay on a coat that appears in *Occasional Desire*. It's called "The Coat." And what moves it isn't digression but interruption. I don't think digression is useless; I just am interested in learning what happens if we suspend our use of it for a while. What would have to appear in its stead? I think I'm thinking with Georges Perec in "The Apartment": "We should learn to live more on staircases, but how?" Or go for sound walks. I'm really just trying to fantasize about a place where the essay might go now and given the exigencies of our contemporary moment.

You know I'm interested in tonal complexity in nonfiction, and the high comic moments in your collection were never lost on me, especially for the way they emerge in the midst of painful material. The keynote of this collection is neither comic nor tragic, though; I think the keynote is your love of irony. There are, of course, self-ironizing tendencies built into the history of the essay, but I wonder if you find yourself working in concert with a particular brand of irony. When it comes to irony, I think Americans as a people (how's that for a generalization?) tend to have tin ears. I tend to think of Americans as not having much of an appetite for irony—I'm not even sure there's a place for it in an American lexicon. Is irony a kind of interruption? Where does it fall on a spectrum that might include smile, grin, or sneer? Is there something implicitly ironic about the character actor?

DL: *Fall* is the right word because for me irony is a kind of verbal slapstick; it's the language of William Demarest, except a bit more complex, borrowing from Stoicism and fatalism and a layered, bemused sense of self, with a

Jewish flavor. The banana peel is there before me in the street, and I think: I see that banana peel there, and my experience tells me that to walk on it would make a fool of myself; I'd slip and fall. So, I can walk around it. Except, knowing me, I'll bump into someone going around the banana peel and accidentally step on it and make things worse. It would be very awkward. Wouldn't it be better just to go ahead and walk on it, take the fall, signal to everyone that I'm not some rube who's never been around a banana peel, and slip and fall but consciously. And then, too, I'll have that experience here on this street. Maybe I can even make something out of it. But I worry about being hurt. I stand there in front of the banana peel. It's getting late. So, I pick up the banana peel and take it home. I figure I can put it down in front of me on the street tomorrow, after I've made a decision.

I wonder if the Italian connection between faggot and aural displacement has to do with sotto voce, or the sub rosa, the sense that one has to, in a queer or taboo subculture, listen more intently somehow. Large ears are a figure of mockery in stories or nursery rhymes. When I was growing up, big ears were always a physiognomic source of potential poking. It's interesting because unlike other male and female appendages that are valued for size, you'd think large ears could be a source of mystical power! But it's all about symmetry, alas . . . Sound is very central to me—like Lamb, who all but admits he's simply wildly neurotic about noise (Schopenhauer has a wonderful essay on noise, and Jacques Attali's book *Noise: The Political Economy of Music* is this wonderful study of music as, well, instrumental sound). I'm hypersensitive to sound, too, though, ironically, I don't want to filter it out as I walk around the city—only at home. I have my students do sound walks too! I use some of the work of the Soundwalk Collective, Soundwalking Interactions, and the work of Hildegard Westerkamp and Janet Cardiff, etc.

I like what you say about the delicacy of lives, such an inescapable and almost perplexing (at least to me) quality. So lovely to see, really, and strange. Of course, who knows what psychological mayhem is ever lurking underneath (you see where I go immediately—I can't let the delicacy be delicate). I'm always a bit like a child around people who are calm and balanced. They're like strangers to me. I don't understand their power.

And *displaced identification* is a wonderful phrase. Michael Strange. I don't know her, but I can understand the fascination. I fixate on characters, obviously, as do you, and then they become my, however you want to call them, patron saints of *strangeness*, or difference. I go through a phase when I examine them minutely—and sometimes I write about them, and sometimes I just need to adopt them or subsume some part of them. Whether it's Elisha Cook Jr. or Dorothy Fields or Dhuoda (author of the medieval mixed-genre handbook, *Liber manualis* [*Handbook for William: A Carolingian Woman's Counsel for Her Son*]).

When we're young we do that with Emily Brontë or Emily Dickinson. It's usually someone named Emily. Occasionally there's a Virginia or someone more obscure. We're sure they're ours and that we've discovered them because usually no one else around is reading this stuff. I was also watching movies and loving things like Eddie Cantor movies and Norma Shearer's strangely awkwardly compelling acting when I was young. This is what makes writers. That impulse to first adopt and understand—the impulse never leaves—to try to thoroughly know. And of course we want to somehow replicate the magic we experience and experienced. Do you remember those first quivering experiences of *Wuthering Heights* or finding Millay in your teens or Yeats?

Maybe this is a good time to shift the focus a bit to talk about teaching, teaching nonfiction specifically and our pedagogies more generally. What I've just been speaking about also, and I'm sure this will sound rather curmudgeonly, reflects an upbringing and much of my adulthood that was less distracted than our day. I mean I read a lot. A lot. For a really long time. I was telling a graduate class that for many years that's what I really did, read for about eight hours a day. But I don't think anyone can do that anymore; it's too terminally distracted an age. I count myself in that indictment too. And I think a lot of work, especially student work, reflects that. I think a lot of the "new" (some of which is not so new) kinds of work, the video essays, etc., may be interesting, but a lot of what's coming out seems to me *distractions of form*. My students also seem distracted by form. They want to know what kind of essay they should write, for example, before they even start writing the essay, which I find somewhat amusing. I do, of course, understand that there is never an absence of form and that form should be inherent and intrinsic. But that's the rub. I suppose I'm finding the need to "play," to "build," to "assemble," to "arrange," crowding out the necessity to go into the hole you speak of (my classes, I admit, are probably more psychodynamic than some others'), and also to write the sentence. To find the way to articulate in that unit boldly, wildly, importantly. I'm getting too many sentences I either don't understand (and I don't mean Susan Howe sentences, in which the poetry of difficulty is a worthy aesthetic, but incomprehensibility) or sentences that seem lame, as though the sentence itself was a kind of afterthought in getting the essay down, which suggests an overvaluation on story or narrative. Actually, a third kind: the "lyrical" sentence, which too often is over-poeticized, frail, or trite. What my students have most trouble with is the declarative sentence.

One more thing I have to say, and I don't care if I get tomatoes thrown at me. A writer in a genre has to know her genre. I've been simply shocked over the years at the number of nonfiction writer-professors who can't talk their way past the last twenty years or so. Oh, they've read Baldwin and Woolf and some Montaigne. Well, they've read Phillip Lopate's anthology. This is extraordinary to me and represents a debasement of what I consider the necessity of the professor's obligation to know her stuff. Who wouldn't be horrified if a poetry professor didn't know Wordsworth, Pope, Dante, Milton? But it's completely common for nonfiction professors to not know Augustine or Rousseau, Johnson or Margery Kempe, Chesterton or Bacon, Julian of Norwich or Twain. Not only does this offend me; it perplexes me. I think some of the hype in nonfiction now about hybridity is that students haven't been taught that it's been around for so long. I'm old-school though. I think students would be better off reading Alice Dunbar-Nelson or Lydia Maria Child, nineteenth-century American essayists, than lots of contemporary memoirs (they aren't mutually exclusive, of course).

Okay, I'm off the soapbox. What do you think? Oh, lest I drive you nuts, I wanted to add something and get your response to it. For a long time I've thought that the nonfiction classroom, which is to say nonfiction pedagogy, is completely under-theorized. I think this is especially true, and crucially true, in the workshop, where we're, like it or not, frequently teaching the autobiographical essay and faced with the shaping of experiences that are dramatic or traumatic, formative, complex, and tender. I have little use for the school of thought that advises that we stick to discussions of art and craft: shaping and shifting, arranging and presentation. In my experience talking about the work requires, frequently, discussion of the experience. And this is, I think, a different skill set for the instructor, in both trying to understand what, experientially, narratively, is required, missing—what the lacunae, yes, the navel, of the essay might be—and how to handle the discussion of it, especially if you have come to understand that, as I mentioned earlier, the psychodynamism of the early drafts of an essay will point to places where the subconscious has indicated subtextually but needs to be made explicit. The workshop can be a very useful place when this happens, and this happens, has happened, in my experience, a whole lot. But it can also be painful. So, I suppose my point is, what is the preparation, what is the pedagogy, for these situations? I'm trying to pull together a class on the psychodynamism of the workshop, but we at least need to be talking and writing about it more. I talk about my many years of therapy in the workshop as a way of letting the class know at least that psychological vulnerability is part of the nature of writing a certain kind of essay and that we need to use different kinds of language, terms of aesthetic criticism and textual analysis along with the language of psychology and affect. I've heard writers of autobiographical essays demur when asked if their work is therapeutic. My response to that is, hell yes. And the workshop is a therapeutic space at times too. But because of what is at stake, it can also be a dangerous space. I think we should consult with psychologists more. All of which is to say, I fantasize about teaching a class with Adam Phillips.

Okay, and in addition to all of that, I want to hear about your new work on mood. Please?

MC: Since these final questions we're approaching are so big, David, I'll start off with a minimalist approach to pedagogy. In thirty words or less the matters that are currently compelling me in the creative nonfiction workshop are the idea of the note and notebook as nonfiction form; the lecture mode of yore that incited a particular type of listener/reader; Cageian silences and other modes of critical nonresistance to the digital world; and nonfiction beyond the page or in performance. That's probably more than thirty words, and I hope it doesn't align me with those "distracted by form."

In your concern about teachers' or students' disinterest in reading or in studying essayistic traditions, I wonder if the problem you are drawing attention to is one of centrism. In spite of global this and that, Americans still enjoy degrees of insulation from or curiosity about anything other than ourselves and what we might call the me-now. Of course, we indulge such centrism to our detriment and the world's. Is a writer or teacher compelled by the short view or the long view, the centrist view or the capacious view?

On the other hand, couldn't it be argued that your history of the essay is not *the* history of the essay? Or that other people might reserve the right to pursue and argue for their own histories of the form? I find that one of the pleasures and beauties of literary nonfiction as a practice is that it encourages the formation of an uncommon archive, a concept that is very important to me: the potentially wide-ranging and unpredictable, sometimes highly privatized and never simply dictated, suite of sources (other texts, ephemera, music, etc.) that we each, so to speak, "consult" when we're at work on a particular composition. Not an obligatory reading list, it's improvisatory, drawn from a wellspring of influences and untapped or unacknowledged sources, including other disciplines.

You are also making me wonder if we're in a terminally distracted age or a terminally fixated one. The *idée fixe*, the stare, the affectless patina that becomes our faces in front of the screen. It's not the first time in the history of the world that humans are suffering from a crisis in attention, in how to notice and what to perceive, in where to locate meaning and how to be attuned to others. I suppose the difference of our age, for any age beset by such a challenge, is how we will make something out of our moment rather than be trapped by it. I have no doubt that what we experience as the "inner life" is shifting and eroding, and I think it will morph into something else by the end of the twenty-first century and after we're long gone. So, too, the sentence and what we think of as an essay's egress to interiority will change either to counter or meet that transformation.

Oh boy, approaching the other big question you raise, the matter of therapy and writing pedagogy, is definitely a thorny area, and I don't want to seem to fall into one camp or another because I really have thought about and dealt with these things a lot, and like you, I try to appreciate their complexity. I think it goes without saying that some writers in my literary nonfiction workshops have life-changing revelations in the course of working in this genre, and they go to places intellectually and emotionally where they've not been before. In the department where I teach, we offer the PhD with creative writing emphasis as well as master's degrees in a program in which the creative writers work closely with scholars and literary theorists too—so we're all about cultivating writers who want that knowledge of literary historical traditions you're concerned about alongside an appetite for critical theory and philosophy. Because the idea of unburdening oneself is already in people's minds when they think of nonfiction, memoir in particular, I'm not keen on the idea of team teaching with a favorite psychoanalyst. On the other hand, Adam Phillips is probably already present in both our classes—insofar as we've internalized so much of his work and thought—and his kind of psychoanalytic thinking is so nuanced, not at all aligned with the conventional notion that we can express ourselves and get free. As my friend Jim Morrison (the writer, not the rock star) likes to say, "There is no catharsis." There's no liberation, just a rearrangement of parts. Because we're such a wound-based culture, a health-obsessed but care-averse culture, admitting therapy as discourse or practice into the creative writing classroom doesn't appeal to me. Nor do the models of either selfhood or writing that attend the idea of writing as a form of healing. Does writing take us to a transformational space? Yes. To a place I want to dwell most of the time? Yes. It's a place where play gets transformed into the best kind of work, and vice versa, but I don't think it's therapeutic. Eating junk food, watching TV, washing dishes, are therapeutic activities for me. They induce a combination of numbness, self-forgetting, self-indulgence, and relaxation that feels good at times.

I'm remembering when I was about a year out from my breast cancer ordeal, telling my oncologist that I'd written a book from it, and her sing-song response: "That must have been very therapeutic for you!" I remember feeling like hitting her when she said that. A lot of other things had been therapeutic—acupuncture, physical therapy, a hairdresser who was also a nurse, etc.—but the writing came from an entirely different place and was addressed to something larger. Was I writing for my life? Maybe. In which case it was beyond therapeutic. It was essential to survival; it was urgent.

The other problem with the writing and therapy connection, I find, is that when it brings healing into play, it can produce a writing that is closed, solved, finished, whereas I think of creative nonfiction as a form of radical openness, like the poetry of Emily Dickinson, or in terms of my friend Mikhail Epstein's definition of the essay: he calls it "a reparative act that isn't closed."

I was teaching Lyn Hejinian's *My Life* recently, and enjoying all over again the possibilities it offers life writing to start with language rather than with experience, to not take anything for granted, including the presumably singular *I* that governs the page. And how it can tempt students to start from someplace else with their autobiographical writing, to give themselves over to a different compositional practices attuned to language: the self as equivalent to the questions that preoccupy it, its life sentences. I think that taking approaches that run athwart mere expression can help writers in our classes to find truths otherwise and, yes, to find a form for formless trauma. Of course all of this depends on the vectors of trust and curiosity that have to be fostered in a workshop's writing community. What would happen if we dispensed with creative nonfiction and literary nonfiction and instead gave each new instantiation of our non-fictive forays the name most suited to the terms of its experimentation? It's that dance of the intellect that my own work aspires to, "lyric intellectual," and that I think Adam Phillips's work achieves.

How's this for a segue? Have you seen Adam Phillips's new piece in *Salmagundi*, "Up to a Point: The Psychoanalyst and the Essay"? "The essayist is the writer who extricates theory from science." That's sort of what I'm doing in the "mood" book I'm currently working on. I've been dreaming this book for a number of years. The impulse behind the book is somewhat similar to *Awkward* insofar as I've chosen to take on a word that is everywhere pervasive but that remains relatively unplumbed. I'm not sure that any of us really knows what we mean when we speak of mood even though we talk about moods in a plethora of contexts—from psychology to politics to aesthetics—and with a variety of consequences. Without pinning mood down, I'm trying to let it take me to unpredictable places and hopefully make something beautiful in the process. Mainly, I want to follow mood as a language rather than reify it as a concept. Something of the wild has to be allowed to come through.

I want to understand the relationship between mood and sound. Moods are absent presences: we can feel them but not locate their source enough to change them. In this sense mood is sound's analog—a perceptible something not readily coeval with its source. I've always been moved by Didier Anzieu's notion of what he calls the "sonorous envelope"—the protective and precarious holding environment (literally, a skin) that is produced for us by the voice of our earliest caretakers. So, voice is important to my excavation—mood as being's envelope or a self's atmosphere—which takes me to weather! How are moods different from climates (over and against the idea that what we take to be the "weather" *affects* our "moods")?

The book is taking on a multi-genre form, perched somewhere between *The Secret Life of Plants* and Roland Barthes's *The Neutral*.

I've been wondering if, in mood's name, I can create a writing that approximates cloudscapes.

And now, David, I must tell you that something happened to me today that signaled the perfect closure for my part of our conversational investigation. I was in the mail room at my university Xeroxing something for my students, when I noticed that one of my colleague's mailboxes was filled to the brim with books. Of course, our mailboxes are all open affairs—a huge wall of cubbyholes. This particular colleague, S., is someone I've learned a great deal from over the years, so when I saw that his mailbox was stacked with books, I really wanted to read their spines. I started to paw through them. I know, this is kind of extraordinary—does it position the essayist as thief? as lurker? as someone who takes liberties? Or is it just that the contents of other people's mailboxes, like their telephone conversations, are simply there for the asking these days? One of the books was a volume of Virginia Woolf's essays, so of course I had to open that one and peruse the table of contents, ever in search of inspiration or the sentence never before glimpsed. And there it was, a little gasp-making phrase at the bottom of her table of contents page, the title of a review essay that appeared in the TLS [*Times Literary Supplement*] in December 1906: it read, "Occasion's Forelock."

For me this closes the mystic circle of our essayistic "interview." So, now can we go for a long walk together at the end of which we arrive at a movie? Or do you need another question? Here's one from that same *Salmagundi* essay, in which Phillips is quoting Woolf. I wonder how you'd answer it: "A novel has a story; a poem rhyme; but what art can the essayist use in these short lengths of prose to sting us wide awake and fix us in a trance which is not sleep but rather an intensification of life—a basking with every faculty alert, in the sun of pleasure?"

DL: The essayist snaps his fingers and raises an eyebrow. He'll actually ask, "Are you with me?" Then, just for your amusement or to give you a sense of what makes her tick, she'll do a little rhythm tap, right on the pavement. He'll say, "Got to love those pronouns." She'll say, please don't tell me where we're headed; let's see where this perambulation takes us. It might be interesting. And then he'll tell the story of the walk later, over a drink.

I do want to just respond to a couple of things before we close. If I seem prescriptive, it certainly isn't about the form the essay might take. Goodness knows I've written enough different kinds of essays and published enough different kinds of essays . . . Montaigne himself was showing off the elasticity of the form in 1580. Nor do I think there's a set list, a comp list, that can't be deviated from in understanding the form. I'm not Allan Blooming it. Though I'm not rejecting the idea of the essay canon either. I think my passion in addressing this topic might be misunderstood for prescription. But I do think it doesn't make any sense to write essays without knowing what *essay* has meant for 450 years. Forms are made to be expanded, to be confounded, to be exploded. If you're going to be serious about the kind of work you want to do and you're going to want to talk about it, I simply can't imagine not knowing your traditions. If that sounds hopelessly old-fashioned, I'm willing to own that. But that doesn't mean I'm arguing for a specific kind of essay. It means I want to argue about the essay with people like you. I suppose I'm supposed to say "discuss," but I'm from Brooklyn.

Essayists have always tried to say what the essay is. It's part of our vocation and our avocation. And we're blissfully doomed to fail. Perhaps that in itself is at the beating heart of the essay.

On the therapeutic value of writing: I think the distinction between catharsis and epiphany is a crucial division for me. Writing *is* a vehicle for cathartic emotional/intellectual play for me, constantly. The release is the ability to say what I haven't been able to say. But epiphanies . . . I'm very suspicious of, and I think they're rare and at best limited. Catharsis is release from repression, finding a way to say what one hasn't been able to, and I think in writing essays one does, if one is lucky, willing, talented, dedicated, despite Jim's imprecation, in my experience, hold that as one of the great possibilities of essay writing. What Jean Starobinski beautifully calls Montaigne's "intuition of the inevitability of change" is the great catharsis that threads through most essays, discovered differently, frequently incompletely, but also often with a liberating lift to the self-capturing consciousness. And therapy for me is dynamic, process oriented (whatever the process is: choose your portion). Not comfort food but an array of dishes spiced to challenge. Whether it heals or not . . . old wounds don't die—they just get more interesting clothing.

About Adam Phillips's comment "The essayist is the writer who extricates theory from science"—I'd prefer to think that the essayist is the writer who integrates theory with art. After all, Mary, you're the gorgeous practitioner of this.

What's compelling me now is just trying to write interesting new essays. Different forms, yes! And some very classical ones. Some even come in the form of conversations. The good conversation is a dance, a pas de deux, and yes, a walk! Who could wish for a better companion than Mary Cappello.

ROCK, PAPER, SCISSORS, GOD

aphorismics

Contradiction is not a sign of falsity, nor the lack of
contradiction a sign of truth.

Little things comfort us because little things distress us.

—BLAISE PASCAL, *PENSÉES*

Our place is somewhere between being
and nonbeing—between two fictions.

—E. M. CIORAN, *ANATHEMAS AND ADMIRATIONS*

ROCK, PAPER, SCISSORS, GOD

Far from the madding crowd—inside it. The flaneur.

Sometimes I need to cross the street to avoid what I'm afraid I might run into if I didn't cross the street.

The city wants you listen to yourself listening to it.

When asked for my street address, I say, "I'm standing right here."

Sometimes my sentences leave their bus passes on the counter. Then they walk around the city until they come to the end of a paragraph.

I have a WALK / DON'T WALK sign on my staircase to prevent accidents between floors.

Is walking a form of public transportation?

One of my earliest memories is riding the trolley in Brooklyn, which ended its run on October 31, 1956, eighty-nine days before I was born.

All night the man upstairs drags a heavy load back and forth. Just as I get to his door to complain, he mutters, "It's a filthy, filthy town."

In the face of all sorts of bestial proclivities, the night-light seems pitch-perfect.

For Halloween the dreamer plays a joke on the dream, by going to bed with a sleep mask.

In the city the person who walks through a crowd crying creates silent havoc. Crying is a virus; you might catch it and die.

While walking down the street, people occasionally used to say, "Smile," to me, and I invariably thought, "Fuck you," about them.

Summer fog wrapping around downtown buildings. You don't know
yourself as well as you thought you did.

The apparition of these faces in the crowd, petals on a wet black cellphone.

He walked through the crowd secretly delighted by the untapped joy of the
passersby.

What do you call those things in doorways that no one ever uses anymore
to scrape off the nighttime city stuff?

The bliss in opening the door and finding no one there.

I used to be a less interesting person than the less interesting person you used to be.

Everyone loves you for the less bothersome version of who you used to be.

Even if you break your mirror and throw away most of the pieces, you can still see your eye, your fingers.

The newest research suggests we should start licking our wounds like cats.

Love is more ironic than you are.

It wasn't a dream. It was a real place. And you and you and you were there. Not you, Alice. You shouldn't even be *here*. Now back to down the hole with you.

And in the end she clicked her red shoes and said, "There's no place like Oz, there's no place like Oz . . ."

There is nothing better than coming home, except for leaving home and staying away from home.

Home is where the range is. The gas range.

Children who can deflect their dysfunctional surroundings grow up to be extraordinarily interesting. Vibratingly damaged in their covering behavior.

Our family crest was a nest of vipers.

It's always a comfort to a talented child to be praised by her psychotic parents.

It's always comforting to make your home feel home-like, a space that almost feels as though you live in it.

I like to surround myself with relics and artifacts of my childhood so my neuroses feel at home.

Even the ghosts that move around my house are filled with tics and phobias. They're worrying themselves to death.

If my closets are full, where do I keep the skeletons?

He loved to argue with himself deep into the night, but when neither side would give in, both left in disgust or despair.

Across the street, in the shadows, walking arm in arm, your nemesis and your doppelganger.

The body is a temple . . . of doom.

If all I have is my health, can I sell it on the black market?

All I have is my health. No resources, interests, friends. I am an excrescence of health.

I'm lucky to have a physician who tests my blood, checks my heart, and vents my spleen.

How many people have you imagined killing today? How many brought back from the dead?

Unless you write your epitaph, you never get the last word.

Sometimes I think all I want is for someone to care about what I was reading when I died. A maudlin thought. No one will know your last thought. Try to make it banal.

Self-epitaph: "He was, they say, not yet dead when he wrote this."

I like to play rock, paper, scissors, God, with God always losing to rock, paper, and scissors.

My son challenges me to make him laugh. I make him laugh. He wants control. He wants to lose control. I want control.

When asked to pick a card, any card, my response is invariably, "Why just one?" I can never leave a premise alone.

I'll only trust a Tarot reading if they tell me something horrible is going to happen immediately.

Walter Benjamin said astrology was for people who are afraid of taking control of their own fate. But what if you're afraid of people who take control of their own fate?

You can't avoid grief; not so, love. Love is completely avoidable.

Theorizing about love is like cooking with a recipe.

We missed the last boat out of Pompeii. So we sat and talked about love.

Last night I dreamed that I couldn't fall asleep at all. I woke up refreshed but ravenous.

Telling one love about another love is like trying to tell lunch that you that didn't have a very good breakfast.

Being in love is like being forced to serve in the Peace Corps in Bali.

I love my family as though they were family.

Some water is thicker than blood.

When love jumped from the thirty-second floor, some people gasped, and some people laughed.

Monogamy is only interesting when it's romantic or aesthetic. Moral monogamy is insipid.

Marriage isn't for the faint of heart. I can't remember where that is on my list of whom marriage isn't for.

On their anniversary they would go visit their uninscribed headstones.

No one knows whether a marriage will last. But divorces have an extraordinary rate of success.

There is an essential difference between baggage and luggage. Try getting a redcap for your baggage.

They say it's darkest before the dawn. But how much before the dawn?

Betrayal should be a game show. Betrayal should be a board game. Betrayal should be the name of a ship. Betrayal should be the name of a wine with no vintage.

I like to be told I'm someone's favorite person, even though I know they tell other people they're their favorite persons. That way I can feel special and betrayed simultaneously.

When someone uses an endearment with me and I then hear them using it with others, I get nauseous.

If you're the cream in my coffee and I like my coffee black, then you're the cream that shouldn't be in my coffee.

When I meet someone and learn they don't drink coffee, I wonder how long they've been celibate.

Tea drinkers are dog lovers, and coffee drinkers love cats. You may be surprised by this, but it is invariably so.

Coffee doesn't keep you awake; it creates the aura of perpetual sunless morning.

Feeling a bit depressed, he asked the barista to grind a bit of him into his expresso as a dark purification ritual.

At the end of the day not even your mother wants you to return from the dead, without conditions.

Hell is where you mostly live; heaven is where you rehab.

The foyer separating heaven and hell has bad air-conditioning.

Mexican saying: I go to heaven for the weather and hell for the company.

What happens when the dark night of the soul is between a rock and a hard place?

Does the soul make a distinction between dark nights and less dark nights?

In the spring the dark nights of the soul end at about 5:00 a.m.

In the dark night of his soul he put the light on so he could better read Saint John of the Cross.

Between a rock and a hard place—but maybe the hard place is a good place.

You can put anything between a rock and a hard place if you move the rock.

He didn't so much skim the surface as surf it.

An aphorism should exhaust itself without exhaustion. If I said anymore, I would just ruin the point. I'd be an aphorism killer. You see?

She wasn't paying any attention at all to his silence, but outside the window he could tell someone was listening.

Some people's conversation is an exuberant ambience, others' a dull white noise.

Sometimes I pay my most severe attention when I'm not listening.

If I could read your lips, I might not read much else.

Twitter and texting—homes for lost aphorisms.

"This is my tweet to the world that has tweeted too much to me."

In the shrinking of texts to suit the stymied attention span, the single letter will one day emerge as the epic.

If you don't change the narrative, the narrative doesn't change.

Teaching the zeitgeist is redundant.

Almost nothing is more ridiculous than trying to contain the infectious pessimism of your position.

I got a box of commas for Christmas, but I think they're stale.

Nothing was as it was supposed to be, and that was how it was supposed to be.

By an underpass of the highway a beat-looking woman was trying to hawk some exclamation marks.

This is the coldest spring since the last very cold spring.

It's not the cold; it's the turbidity.

The neighborhood has really gone downhill since it gentrified.

My new neighbors are named "Nodule."

My neighbors' silences drive me to complain to the superintendent.

When I see a glimpse of friendliness in my neighbors' eyes, I'm filled with anxiety.

"I wouldn't be caught dead . . ." If I were caught dead, I wouldn't particularly care.

My neighbors are very respectable, very bourgeois zombies. They read the *Times* before they head out in the morning.

My zombie neighbors invited me to a potluck. I didn't want to go, but they twisted my arm.

I have Jewish zombie neighbors. I wasn't sure if they were kosher, but then I saw that they had two sinks.

The current fascination with zombies is just a longing for unrepentant cannibalism.

Reached out of a dream to put my glasses on, wanting to see why my mother's robe wasn't green anymore.

Took off my glasses in the middle of the night, tired of a dream, its excesses.

An aphorism is a cul-de-sac that you aren't unhappy you drove down.

Most of the time when we ask someone to repeat something, it isn't because we haven't heard what they said. It's because we want the power to ventriloquize them.

I don't remember anyone's name because when I meet them, I'm struggling so hard to remember my own.

Having the last word is empty: emptiness follows the last word.

MOTHERS, ETC.

Illustrations by Heather Frise

The arc of a Mother is equal to two times the square root of what you dreamed between the ages of twelve and fifteen.

The Mothers were always better sailors at night.

In olden days Mothers would let their children handle all the perilous dancing.

In pairs the Mothers danced out of the kissing school for recess.

On the street yesterday all the Mothers were looking at me strangely.

Most of my Mothers died ages ago, though a few of them linger on, here and there.

Some people swear they've never seen a Mother, and others see them on the undersides of airplanes or in the little glass cases at the automat.

Mothers are birds that can't stand still.

The nectar of a Mother feeds more than a two-edged bird.

Even among the cirrus and cumulus, hungry mouths would appear.

Mothers remember that they are birds, when birds knew how to dance.

The Mothers told us what we were most afraid of before putting us in a nice warm bath.

Mothers of twins wait for the next blue moon.

Most of the Mothers dressed as their fathers for Halloween, while a few dressed as their mothers dressed as their fathers.

Sometimes, out of nowhere, a Mother will love herself in a darkly consoling way.

At the party for the Mothers the mirrors were doing some strange things to the lights, and the lights were doing some strange things to the mirrors.

She had heard that blood was so good for the skin, that Mother.

Only Mothers are allowed to look at the sun directly since love is such a dark-eyed thing.

Before the Mothers trays of sweetmeats and snap traps. Behind them changelings and black fog.

Mothers command you to pull over and park.

Every August the Mothers disappeared, leaving the children to sail, eat ice cream, and compose songs that sounded like laughing Mothers keening.

During aperitifs Mothers' hands drift under their dresses, and the piano player pretends he's swimming.

The Mothers climbed over the town walls at night because that's when
hardly anyone noticed them.

Mothers: their legs were creamy white, and they always wore sling backs.

All the Mothers said in unison that it was time to draw the blinds in the parlor.

When the bird's heart was found in the shallow water, two of the Mothers swam far away.

The question of which came first, the Mother or the egg, has always bored me.

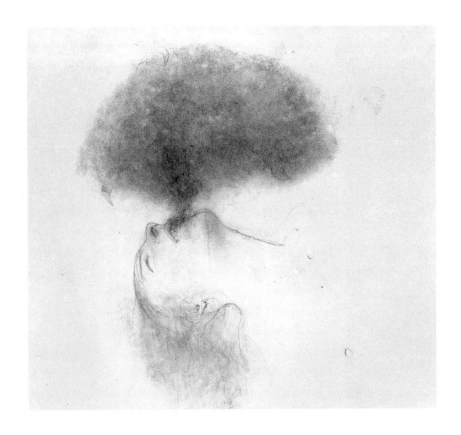

You can get addicted to a Mother, even if she isn't your own.

Neither the Mothers nor the trees could decide what the wind wanted.

The yellow leaves will fall around Mothers, for all Mothers are fallen, and sometimes we find our Mothers when we aren't even looking for them, like when we're looking out the window or going to the tearoom or swimming out too far.

In the native language *mother* was a synonym for *monsoon, soft wood,* and the extra bit of skin near the neck or knees.

The Mothers carried buckets of red sand to protect themselves against lies and trees that tried to grow hurtfully from the sky.

The entire tea service set out by the Mothers was cracked and chipped.

Before flying off for warmer climes, Mothers will sometimes do a cancan, though they're thinking of a *danse primitif, danse sauvage.*

Sometimes a Mother will burst into flames in a dream in which her past or yours seems uncontainable.

The Mothers performed a dance that was called the "fire song"; all the men wept openly, and the children escaped.

To this day some are sure it really says, "Am I my Mother's keeper?"

Mothers are always hungrier than you think.

The Mothers gathered around and whispered in my ear, but I told them to let the highest waves break and stop taking your name in vain.

Mothers laugh at you behind your back and draw cruel caricatures of your desires.

Mothers freeze-dry our tears and sell them on the black market.

Necessity was the Mother of my great aunt, who was not very nice.

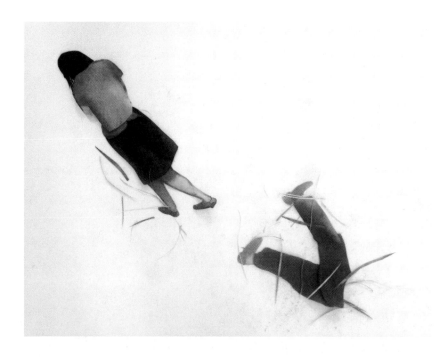

But surely you've always known that a Mother will often weep when the
pants turn up facedown in the bulrushes.

A Mother with a monkey on her back is no less a Mother than a Mother who has never had a monkey.

The Mother couldn't help holding what she carried.

The Mothers would climb the tallest buildings in reasonably appropriate attire.

Mothers find all your secret hiding places, sometimes to their dismay.

The Mothers' faces looked down on the rest of their bodies with a combination of pity and hilarity.

At the auction last night near the Black Forest, one of the Mothers sold for seven hundred dollars.

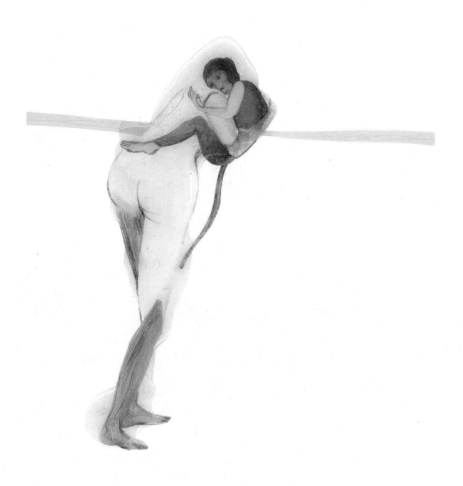

To many Mothers there is a species of delight in the burden of merging identities with what we euphemistically call their offspring.

The Mothers in the mezzanine were wearing vermillion, while those in the balcony preferred folly.

When Mothers jump so high, kitchen bloodred, bathroom Feldgrau,
bedroom black.

Mothers of Mothers know about places even all the other Mothers don't know about.

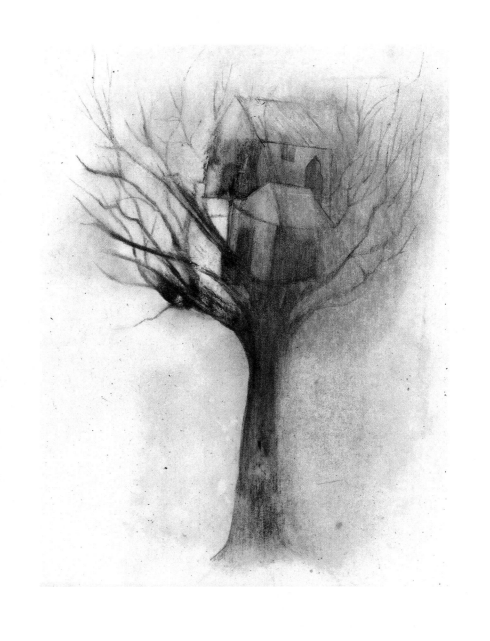

Someone once told me he had seen one of the Mothers on a night when Mothers are susceptible to being seen. He said she was nacreous, a ship waiting in the harbor.

SOURCE CREDITS

Lee Adams and Charles Strouse. "Honestly Sincere." 1960. © Peermusic Publishing, Warner/Chappell Music, Inc.

Dante Alighieri. "Inferno XI." In *The Divine Comedy*. New York: Vintage, 2013.

Harold Arlen and E. Y. Harburg. "If I Only Had a Brain." 1939.

W. H. Auden. "Sept. 1, 1939." In *Another Time*. New York: Random House, 1940.

The Barbarians. "Moulty." © Homefield Music, Sony ATV Music Pub LLC, Spirit Music Group.

Samuel Barber and James Agee. *Knoxville: Summer of 1915*. Copyright ©1949 (Renewed) by G. Schirmer, Inc. (ASCAP) This arrangement © 2017 by G. Schirmer, Inc. (ASCAP) International copyright secured. All rights reserved. Used by permission.

Roland Barthes. *Roland Barthes*. New York: Hill & Wang, 1977.

Charles Baudelaire. "Au Lecteur." In *Les Fleurs du mal*. Paris: Auguste Poulet-Malassis, 1857.

Robert Burton. *The Anatomy of Melancholy*, 16th ed. London: B. Blake, 1838.

Bob Crewe and Bob Gaudio. "Walk Like a Man." 1963. © Sony/ATV Music Publishing LLC, Kobalt Music Publishing Ltd.

Dhuoda. "Book Ten: 1. On the Age You Have Obtained" and "Book Ten: 2. On the verses I have begun with the letters of your name." In *The Handbook for William: A Carolingian Woman's Counsel for Her Son*. Washington DC: The Catholic University of America Press, 1999.

Emily Dickinson. "'Hope' is the thing with feathers." In *The Poems of Emily Dickinson*, edited by R. W. Franklin. Cambridge MA: Harvard University Press, 1999.

Dion and the Belmonts. "Runaround Sue." 1961. Written by Dion Di Mucci, Ernie Maresca. Copyright © Sony/ATV Music Publishing LLC, Warner/Chappell Music, Inc, The Bicycle Music Company, Music Sales Corporation.

John Earle. "Acquaintance." In *The World Display'd: Or, Several Essays*. 1740.

The Four Seasons. "Walk Like a Man." Vee-Jay Records. 1963.

Herman's Hermits. "Mrs. Brown, You've Got a Lovely Daughter," MGM. 1965.

Joe Hill. "The Preacher and the Slave." In *The Little Red Songbook*, 1911.

Al Jolson, Billy Rose, and Dave Dreyer. "Me and My Shadow." 1927. © Memory Lane Music Group, Bourne Co.

Jerome Kern and Dorothy Fields. "Never Gonna Dance." 1936. © Universal Music Publishing Group, Shapiro Bernstein & Co. Inc.

Jerome Kern and Dorothy Fields. "The Way You Look Tonight." 1936. © Universal Music Publishing Group, Shapiro Bernstein & Co. Inc.

Charles Lamb. "A Character of the Late Elia." In *Essays of Elia*. Philadelphia: Carey, Lea, and Carey, 1828.

David Lazar. "Being a Boy-Man." In *Being: What Makes a Man*, ed. Jill McCabe Johnson. Lincoln, NE: University of Nebraska Gender Programs, 2014.

Ewan MacColl. "The First Time Ever I Saw Your Face." Published by Bucks Music Group Limited, administered by The Royalty Network. Used by permission.

Michel de Montaigne. "To the Reader." In *Essays of Michel de Montaigne*. Translated by Charles Cotton. France: Simon Millanges, Jean Richer, 1580.

Trevor Peacock. "Mrs. Brown, You've Got a Lovely Daughter." 1965. © Warner/ Chappell Music, Inc.

Florence Reece. "Which Side Are You On." 1931. © The Bicycle Music Company.

Beverly Ross and Julius Dixon. "Lollipop." Used by permission of Edward B. Marks Music Company.

Peggy Seeger. "I'm Gonna Be An Engineer." 1979. © The Bicycle Music Company.

Stephen Sondheim. "Being Alive" and "Someone Is Waiting." Used by permission of Herald Square Music, Inc., on behalf of Range Road Music, Inc., Jerry Leiber Music, Silver Seahorse Music LLC and Rilting Music Inc.

Gerald Stern. "Lillian Harvey." In *Lovesick Poems*. New York: Harper & Row, 1987.

Wallace Stevens. "An Ordinary Evening in New Haven." In *The Auroras of Autumn*. New York: Knopf, 1950.

Mark Strand. "Keeping Things Whole." *Selected Poems*. New York: Knopf, 1979, 1980.

Charles Strouse and Lee Adams. "Honestly Sincere." 1960.

Pete Townshend. "I'm a Boy." Hampshire House Publishing Corporation, TRO Essex Music Group. Used by permission.

Butch Walker. "I Love You." 1962. © Sony/ATV Music Publishing LLC, Universal Music.